C000129101

SAMS TEA
WINDOWS NT
WORKSTATION 4
IN
10
MINUTES

Sue Plumley and Paul Cassel

SAMS

201 West 103rd St., Indianapolis, Indiana 46290 USA

SAMS TEACH YOURSELF WINDOWS NT WORKSTATION 4 IN 10 MINUTES

Copyright © 1999 by Sams Publishing

International Standard Book Number: 0-672-31580-7

Library of Congress Catalog Card Number: 98-89463

Printed in the United States of America

First Printing: February 1999

01   00   99   4   3   2

TRADEMARKS

All terms mentioned in this book that are known to be trade-marks or service marks have been appropriately capitalized. Sams Publishing cannot attest to the accuracy of this information. Use of a term in this book should not be regarded as affecting the validity of any trademark or service mark. Windows NT® Work-station 4 is a registered trademark of Microsoft Corporation.

WARNING AND DISCLAIMER

Every effort has been made to make this book as complete and as accurate as possible, but no warranty or fitness is implied. The information provided is on an *as is* basis. The authors and the publisher shall have neither liability nor responsibility to any person or entity with respect to any loss or damages arising from the information contained in this book.

Executive Editor

Grace Buechlein

Development Editor

Laura Bulcher

Managing Editor

Brice Gosnell

Project Editor

Sara Bosin

Copy Editor

Pamela Woolf

Indexers

Debra Myers
Christine Nelson

Proofreader

Andrew Beaster

Technical Editor

Jeff Nickles

Interior Design

Gary Adair

Cover Design

Aren Howell

Layout Technician

Michael J. Poor

CONTENTS AT A GLANCE

TABLE OF CONTENTS

ABOUT THE AUTHORS

Sue Plumley is the owner and operator of a business that provides training, consulting, and network installation, management, and maintenance to banking, education, medical, and industrial facilities. She has authored and co-authored over 70 books for Macmillan Computer Publishing.

Paul Cassel is a software consultant who has extensive experience in using and testing Windows NT and various other Microsoft products. He is the author of *Using Windows NT Workstation 4* and co-author of several other Macmillan Computer Publishing titles. Paul has won numerous MVP awards from Microsoft and similar awards and recognition from other software companies.

DEDICATIONS

Dedicated to my dad, Ovis L. "John" Bender—Sue Plumley

This book is dedicated to the Tirilee—Paul Cassel

TELL US WHAT YOU THINK!

As the reader of this book, *you* are our most important critic and commentator. We value your opinion and want to know what we're doing right, what we could do better, what areas you'd like to see us publish in, and any other words of wisdom you're willing to pass our way.

As an executive editor for the Operating Systems team at Macmillan Computer Publishing, I welcome your comments. You can fax, email, or write me directly to let me know what you did or didn't like about this book—as well as what we can do to make our books stronger.

Please note that I cannot help you with technical problems related to the topic of this book, and that due to the high volume of mail I receive, I might not be able to reply to every message.

When you write, please be sure to include this book's title and author as well as your name and phone or fax number. I will carefully review your comments and share them with the author and editors who worked on the book.

Fax: 317.581.4663

Email: opsys@mcp.com

Mail: Executive Editor
            Operating Systems
            Macmillan Computer Publishing
            201 West 103rd Street
            Indianapolis, IN 46290 USA

INTRODUCTION

Windows NT 4 provides a powerful yet easy-to-use operating system that enables you to use a variety of applications in addition to connecting to a variety of networks. The features and procedures of Windows NT are similar to those of Windows 95, but the power behind the application is supreme.

THE WHAT AND WHY OF WINDOWS NT WORKSTATION 4

Windows NT 4 is an exceptional operating system that enables you to perform tasks—such as opening programs, copying files, editing documents, and so on—that help you get your work done quickly and easily. In addition, Windows NT lets you connect to your company's network to access other computers, files, printers, and more.

Windows NT is a *graphical user interface* (GUI), which means that Windows provides a workspace that is graphical, and therefore, easy to use and easy to understand. As you become familiar with Windows NT, you'll find that it makes it easy to use applications effectively to manage your files.

Graphical User Interface A GUI (pronounced "gooey") makes interacting with your computer easy. You usually use a mouse to point at and select icons (small pictures that represent files or application programs), and you choose operations (commands from menus) to perform on those icons. A GUI is an alternative to a command-line interface such as DOS, where the user must enter text commands from the keyboard. Windows NT also incorporates a command-line interface (CLI) that is available when you need it.

Why use Windows NT? Windows NT makes using your computer faster and easier in the following ways:

- You can work in and have several applications open on-screen at the same time if you like. You can also easily switch between open applications and share data between applications.

- The graphical user interface is easy to understand and use, so you'll be up and running quickly. Once you get started, you'll be surprised at how quickly your "educated guesses" become correct choices.

- All application programs designed for Windows NT look similar: the title bars, menus, icons, and commands are often comparable. In addition, Windows applications use similar keyboard and mouse operations to select objects and choose commands. To a great extent, once you've learned one application, you've learned them all.

- You can integrate with a variety of servers, including UNIX, NetWare, TCP/IP, Windows NT Server, and MS LAN Manager.

- You can use either 16-bit and 32-bit applications.

- Video and graphics applications run smoothly so that multimedia applications, games, and graphics programs such as CorelDRAW! really shine.

Windows NT's GUI provides a common approach to using a variety of applications for your computer. Learning Windows NT is fast, easy, and fun—and it takes little effort.

WHY THE *SAMS TEACH YOURSELF WINDOWS NT WORKSTATION 4 IN 10 MINUTES?*

Sams Teach Yourself Windows NT Workstation 4 in 10 Minutes will save you time. Each lesson is designed so that you can complete it in 10 minutes or less, so you'll be up-to-snuff in basic Windows skills quickly.

Although you can jump between lessons, starting at the beginning is a good plan. The bare-bones basics are covered first, followed by more advanced topics. Whatever you do, don't miss the inside front and back covers. The inside front cover of this book features a list of common Windows NT Workstation tasks. The inside back cover contains a typical Windows NT screen and points out its common elements.

CONVENTIONS USED IN THIS BOOK

To help you move through the lessons easily, this book uses the following conventions:

On-screen text	On-screen text appears in bold type.
What you type	Information you type appears in bold color type.
Items you select	Commands, options, and icons you select as well as keys you press appear in color type.

In telling you to choose menu commands, this book uses the format *menu name, menu command*. For example, "choose File, Properties," means "open the File menu and select the Properties command."

In addition to these conventions, the *Sams Teach Yourself Windows NT Workstation 4 in 10 Minutes* uses the following icons to identify helpful information:

Plain English tips define new terms or terms that may be unfamiliar to you, such as technical terminology, jargon, and so on.

Tips include keyboard and mouse shortcuts and hints that can save you time and energy.

Caution icons identify areas where new users often run into trouble, and offer practical solutions to those problems.

TRADEMARKS

All terms mentioned in this book that are known to be trademarks have been appropriately capitalized. Sams cannot attest to the accuracy of this information. Use of a term in this book should not be regarded as affecting the validity of any trademark or service mark.

Navigating the Windows NT Desktop

In this lesson, you'll learn how to start and shut down Windows NT, how to work with the parts of the Windows NT desktop, and how to use a mouse to manipulate items on the desktop.

Starting Windows NT Workstation

To start Windows NT Workstation, turn your computer and monitor on. What happens next depends on how your computer is *configured* (set up). The NT Loader screen appears, offering you various options to start the computer. If, for example, your computer is configured for a *dual boot*, you can select the operating system you want to use for the current session (for example, Windows NT, MS-DOS, or Windows 98). If you're using only the Windows NT operating system, you can leave the computer alone and let the default Windows NT operating system start on its own.

Dual Boot A dual boot is a setup option that allows you to use either the Windows NT Workstation operating system to run your computer, or another operating system such as DOS or Windows 98. The NT Loader screen presents your options, and you choose one by pressing the up or down arrow on the keyboard and pressing Enter to confirm your choice.

If NT is your only operating system, the computer runs through its general startup and then displays the Windows NT

Workstation *Welcome* screen. Behind the Welcome message box, you'll see the NT logo and the blank desktop.

Follow these steps to log on to Windows NT:

1. Press and hold the Ctrl key then press and hold the Alt key, and finally press the Delete key. Release all three keys, and the second Welcome screen appears.

2. Enter the following information. If you're unsure of any answer, ask your system administrator.

    Username   The name you want to use to log on to the network.

    From   The name of your computer on the network. This box might already have a name in it. If so, enter the name of your workgroup or domain only if the one already there is incorrect.

    Domain   Allows you to select the domain to which you log on. May appear instead of From.

    Password   Your password to get into your computer and on to the network.

Error Message   Many different errors could occur at this point. For example, a message might appear on your screen telling you that the connection could not be restored or that you're not a valid user. First, make sure you've typed your password correctly. If you still have a problem connecting to the network, see your system administrator for help.

3. Press Enter to log on to the network. The NT desktop appears.

Keyboard Shortcut   Pressing Enter in a dialog or message box is the same as choosing the OK button; pressing the Escape key is the same as choosing Cancel

UNDERSTANDING THE WINDOWS NT DESKTOP

After Windows NT is installed on your system, the Windows NT desktop appears each time you start your computer. As you can see in Figure 1.1, the Windows NT screen is made up of many components. These components enable you to open applications, manage files, send and receive email, and perform many other tasks throughout your work day.

FIGURE 1.1   Common components of the Windows NT screen and an open My Computer window.

The components of the NT screen include

> **Desktop**   This is the background on which all other elements appear. You can think of the Windows NT desktop like the top of your own traditional office desk. Just as you can move papers around, hide certain items in drawers, and add and remove things on your desk, you can manipulate things on your NT desktop.

> **My Computer**   The My Computer icon represents the contents of your computer, including the hard drive, floppy and CD drives, applications, folders, files, and so on. Double-click an icon to open it and view its contents; the My Computer window in Figure 1.1 shows the contents of the My Computer icon. Double-click any icon in the window to view its contents.

> **Network Neighborhood**   This icon displays other computers connected to your computer either on a Microsoft network such as NT or Windows for Workgroups, or on another network, such as Novell NetWare.

> **Inbox**   The Inbox represents Microsoft Exchange, a program you can use to fax and email other computers.

> **Internet Explorer**   If you have access to an Internet service provider (ISP), you can use the Internet Explorer to access the Net, including Web pages and email.

> **Recycle Bin**   The Recycle Bin is a place in which deleted objects remain until you empty the trash. You can retrieve items—files, programs, pictures, and so on—from the Recycle Bin after you delete them. Once you empty the trash, however, you can no longer retrieve items from the bin.

> **My Briefcase**   My Briefcase is a special feature you can use for copying and transferring files from your computer to a portable computer. My Briefcase enables you to easily transfer and update your files.

Windows   Windows are boxed areas that contain icons representing drives and other hardware, folders (or directories), applications, files, and so on. You can open, close, size, move, and otherwise manipulate windows, as well as add and remove icons from a window.

Title bar   The title bar of any window displays the name of the window. For example, the name of the My Computer window appears in the My Computer title bar. Additionally, the title bar includes three buttons you can use to manipulate the window (you'll learn about them in Lesson 2, "Working with a Window").

Menu bar   The menu bar contains the menus of commands you choose in order to perform procedures or actions within any application displaying a menu. When you open a menu, a list of related commands appears (see Lesson 3, "Using Menus").

Icons   Icons are pictures that represent programs (Microsoft Excel, WordPerfect), files (documents, spreadsheets, graphics), printer information (setup options, installed fonts), computer information (hard and floppy disk drives), and so on in both Windows NT and Windows applications. Most often, you use icons to launch programs and open folders and files (as you'll learn in Lesson 2).

Taskbar   The taskbar contains the Start button, any open application or window buttons, and the System Tray. You can click a taskbar button to open the window or application it represents.

Start Button   The Start button displays a menu from which you can choose to open an application, open a document, customize NT, find a file or folder, access help files, or shut down Windows NT.

Folder   A folder contains files and other folders on your computer; for example, the Printers folder includes icons representing your printer(s) and an application for adding a printer to your system. A folder is the same thing as a directory.

Pointer The pointer is an onscreen icon (usually an arrow) that represents your mouse, trackball, touchpad, or
other selecting device. You use it to select items and choose
commands. You move the pointer by moving the mouse or
other device. You'll learn how to use the mouse in the next
section.

USING THE MOUSE

You use the mouse to perform many actions in Windows NT and
in Windows applications. With the mouse, you can easily select
an icon, folder, or window, among many other things. Selecting
involves two steps: pointing and clicking. You can also open icons
and folders by double-clicking them, and you can move an item
by clicking and dragging it.

To *point* to an object (icon, window title bar, and so on), move
the mouse across your desk or mouse pad until the onscreen
mouse pointer touches the object. You can pick up the mouse and
reposition it if you run out of room on your desk. To *click*, point
the mouse pointer at the object you want to select, and then press
and release the left mouse button. If the object is an icon or window, it becomes highlighted. When following steps in this book,
click the left mouse button unless the directions specify otherwise.

The right mouse button can be used when you want to display
a shortcut menu. To *right-click*, point the mouse pointer at an
object—folder, taskbar, desktop, window, and so on—and click
the right mouse button. A shortcut menu that presents common
commands relating to the object appears. If, for example, you
right-click a folder, the menu might offer these commands: Open ,
Explore , Create Shortcut , and Properties . The items on the menu
depend on the object you're right-clicking.

When you *double-click* an item, you point to the item and press
and release the left mouse button twice quickly. Double-clicking
is often a shortcut to performing a task. For example, you can
open a window or folder by double-clicking its icon.

You can use the mouse to move an object (usually a window, dialog box, or icon) to a new position onscreen. You do this by *clicking and dragging* the object. To drag an object to a new location onscreen, point to the object, press and hold the left mouse button, move the mouse to a new location, and release the mouse button. The object moves with the mouse cursor as you drag it.

You can also perform certain actions, such as selecting multiple items or copying items, by performing two additional mouse operations. *Shift+click* means to press and hold the Shift key, and then click the left mouse button; *Ctrl+click* means to press and hold the Ctrl key, and then click the left mouse button. The result of either of these actions depends on where you are in Windows NT.

USING THE START BUTTON

The Windows NT Start button provides access to programs and documents, the Help feature, the Find feature, and many other elements in NT. You'll use the Start button to perform most tasks in Windows. For more information about using menus, see Lesson 3.

To use the Start button, follow these steps:

1. Point the mouse at the Start button, located on the taskbar, and click the button. The Start menu appears (see Figure 1.2).

2. Click the task or command you want to display, as follows:

   Programs   Displays Windows Accessories programs, administrative tools, applications, the Command Prompt program, and so on.

   Documents   Displays up to 15 of the most recently opened documents. For quick and easy access, click the document name and the document and the associated application opens.

Click here
to begin.——

FIGURE 1.2   The Start menu provides easy access to programs.

Settings   Displays the Control Panel and Printers folders and the Taskbar command for customizing your Windows NT setup. For more information, see Lesson 26, "Controlling the Hardware Settings".

Find   Enables you to search for specific files, folders, and computers. You can search your own hard drive or the network drive.

Help   Displays help for performing tasks and procedures in NT. For more information, see Lesson 5, "Using Windows NT Help".

Run   Enables you to enter a command (such as A:\install) to run a program from hard disks, floppy disks, or CD-ROMs.

Shut Down   Displays the Shut Down dialog box in which you prepare your computer to be turned off.

Cascading Menu? An arrow after any menu command means another menu, called a *cascading* or sub-menu, will appear if you point to that command. NT supplies as many as four cascading menu layers starting from the Start menu.

USING THE TASKBAR

In addition to the Start button, the taskbar displays buttons representing open windows and applications. You can quickly switch to another window or application by clicking its button on the taskbar. Figure 1.3 shows the taskbar with two buttons: My Computer (representing the open My Computer window) and Exploring (representing the hidden, or minimized, Windows Explorer).

You can move the taskbar to the top, left, or right side of the screen to customize your workspace. Additionally, you can hide the taskbar until you need it.

To move the taskbar, click the mouse anywhere on the bar except on a button and drag the taskbar to the right, the left, or the top of the screen. As you drag, the taskbar relocates to that area. You can easily drag the taskbar back to the bottom if you prefer it there. For help on using menus and dialog boxes, see Lessons 3 and 4.

To hide the taskbar, follow these steps:

1. Choose the Start button.

2. From the Start menu, choose Settings, and then choose Taskbar. The Taskbar Properties sheet appears (see Figure 1.3).

3. Choose the Auto Hide check box by clicking that box; then press Enter to close the dialog box. The taskbar slides off the screen.

FIGURE 1.3   You can choose to hide the taskbar when you're not using it.

When you need the taskbar, move the mouse to where the taskbar was; you may have to slide the mouse off of the screen. The taskbar reappears.

 Show Taskbar   To show the taskbar all the time, choose Start, Settings, Taskbar, and click the Auto Hide check box so no check mark appears. Press Enter to close the dialog box.

SHUTTING DOWN WINDOWS NT

Before you turn off your computer, you must shut down Windows NT properly to ensure that you don't lose any data or configuration changes. Lesson 7, "Shutting Down Windows NT" describes shutting down in more detail. To quickly shut down Windows NT, follow these steps:

1. Press and hold the Alt key, and then press and release the
   F4 key. Release the Alt key. First, the open windows and
   applications close, one at a time. When all open windows
   are closed, the Shut Down Windows dialog box appears.

2. Choose Shut down the Computer? by clicking its option.

3. Press the Enter key or choose Yes, and Windows NT begins the process of shutting down. When NT displays a
   message saying you can safely turn off your computer,
   you can turn off both the monitor and the computer.

In this lesson, you learned about the parts of the Windows NT
desktop and how to use the mouse to manipulate items on the
desktop. In the next lesson, you'll learn how to work with
windows.

2 WORKING WITH A WINDOW

In this lesson, you'll learn how to open, resize, move, view, and close a window. You'll also learn how to use scrollbars to view more of a window.

WHAT IS A WINDOW?

A *window* is a boxed area in which you view files, folders, drives, hardware icons, or other elements. Figure 2.1 shows the components that make up a window. Many of these components are the same for all windows in Windows NT and Windows applications, which makes it easy for you to manage your work.

You can open and close a window, reduce and enlarge a window, and move a window around—which is what this lesson is all about. In addition, you can open more than one window at a time, stack one window on top of another, and otherwise manipulate windows as explained in Lessons 8, "Working with Multiple Windows," and 9, "Copying and Moving Information Between Windows".

Table 2.1 briefly describes the common elements of a window. Keep in mind that although most windows are similar, you will run across some windows that do not have all these elements.

FIGURE 2.1   The elements of a typical window.

TABLE 2.1   WINDOW ELEMENTS

ELEMENT	DESCRIPTION
Title bar	Contains the Control menu and the Minimize, Maximize, Restore, and the Close buttons, and may contain the window's name.
Menu bar	Contains menus with related commands and options that help you control the window and its contents. See additional information about menus in Lesson 3, "Using Menus".

continues

TABLE 2.1 **CONTINUED**

ELEMENT	DESCRIPTION
Control menu button	Contains commands that help you manage the window itself.
Toolbar	Graphic tool buttons that represent shortcuts to various menu commands. For more information, see Lesson 3.
Minimize button	A button that reduces the window to a button on the toolbar.
Maximize button	A button that enlarges the window to fill the screen.
Close button	A button that closes the window.
Folders	Icons that represent directories; folders can hold other folders and files.
Files	Documents, spreadsheets, databases, programs, and other components stored in folders on a drive in your computer.
Window border	A rim around a restored window (discussed later in this lesson) that you can use to resize the window.
Status bar	A bar across the bottom of the window that provides information such as free space on a drive, number of objects or files in a window, and so on.
Scrollbar	A vertical or horizontal bar that enables you to view hidden areas of a window.

No Toolbar or Status bar? If a window doesn't display the toolbar, choose the View menu, Toolbar command; to display the status bar, choose View, Status Bar.

WINDOWS CONTENTS

NT is made up of many types of windows that often contain different items. Each icon on your desktop when opened, for example, displays different contents just as various folders, files, and applications display various contents. Additionally, after you open a window you can usually open items within the window, such as icons, folders, programs, and documents. Often, you can open a window within a window within a window, and so on, until your desktop is filled with windows.

The following is an example of a set of windows you can open from the My Computer icon:

My Computer window Displays hard drive icons, floppy disk and CD icons, Control Panel folder (containing icons for customizing NT) and the Printers folder (containing an icon representing your printer).

Hard drive icon Displays all folders (or directories) on that drive, plus any files found on the root directory (usually drive C).

Program Files folder Displays folders representing programs installed on your computer.

Newtwork Neighborhood Displays resources on your network.

OPENING A WINDOW

To open a window from an icon, double-click the icon. For example, point at the My Computer icon and double-click it. If you do it correctly, the My Computer icon opens into the My Computer window.

Double-Click Trouble? If you have trouble opening a window by double-clicking, you need to practice the double-click movement. You can also change the speed of the double-click to better suit your "trigger" finger; see Lesson 26, "Controlling the Hardware Settings" for more information.

There is another method you can use to open a window. Just point to the icon and right-click once, and a shortcut menu appears. Select Open from the menu to open the window.

SIZING A WINDOW WITH MAXIMIZE, MINIMIZE, AND RESTORE

You may want to increase the size of a window to see its full contents, or you may want to decrease a window to a button on the taskbar in order to make room for other windows. You can use the Maximize, Minimize, and Restore buttons located at the right end of the window's title bar, or you can use the Maximize, Minimize, and Restore commands on the Control menu. The buttons and the commands work as follows:

 Select the Maximize button or command to enlarge the window. A maximized My Computer window, for example, fills your entire screen, thus hiding any of the desktop in the background. Clicking the Maximize button of a program, document, or any other window enlarges it to fill the screen.

Select the Minimize button or command to reduce the window to a button on the taskbar.

 Select the Restore button or command to return a window to the size it was before it was maximized. (The Restore button and command are available only after a window has been maximized; the Restore button replaces the Maximize button on the title bar in a maximized window.)

Figure 2.2 shows the My Computer window maximized; it fills the entire desktop. At full size, the My Computer window's Restore button is available. When it's any other size, you see the Maximize button instead of the Restore button.

FIGURE 2.2 The My Computer window enlarges to fill the screen.

To maximize, minimize, or restore a window, click the appropriate button on the title bar. You can also maximize, minimize, or restore a window with the keyboard, using these steps:

1. Click the Control menu button to open the window's Control menu; or alternatively, press Alt+Spacebar.

2. Click the command (Restore, Minimize, or Maximize) you want to initiate. Alternatively, use the down arrow to move to and highlight the command, then press Enter.

Sizing a Window's Borders

At some point, you'll need a window to be a particular size to suit your needs. For example, you might want to fit two or more windows onscreen at the same time. You can drag the window's frame or border to change the size of the window. A window frame appears only on a restored window, not on a maximized or minimized window.

To resize a window, follow these steps:

1. Place the mouse pointer on the border of the window that you want to resize. When the mouse pointer is positioned correctly, it changes into one of these three shapes:

    The vertical double-headed arrow appears when you position the mouse pointer over the top or bottom window frame. It enables you to resize the window's height by dragging the frame up or down.

    The horizontal double-headed arrow appears when you position the mouse pointer over the right or left side of the window frame. It enables you to resize the window's width by dragging the frame left or right.

    The diagonal double-headed arrow appears when you position the mouse pointer over any of the four corners of the window frame. It enables you to resize the window's height and width proportionally by dragging the corner diagonally.

2. Click and drag the border toward the center of the window to reduce the window, or drag away from the center to enlarge the window.

3. When the border reaches the desired location, release the mouse button.

USING SCROLLBARS

Scrollbars appear along the bottom or the right edge of a window when a window contains more text, graphics, or icons than it can display at its current size.

Using scrollbars, you can move up, down, left, or right in a window. Figure 2.3 shows an example. Because all the hard drive window's contents are not fully visible in the window, the scrollbars are present on the right side and bottom of the window.

FIGURE 2.3   Use scrollbars to move within the window.

What's a Scrollbar?   A *scrollbar* is a bar that contains three items: two scroll arrows and a scroll box. You use the scroll arrows and the scroll box to move around in the window, scrolling a line at a time, or even a page at a time.

The following steps teach you how to use the scrollbars to view items not visible in the window:

1. To see an object that is down and to the right of the viewable area of the window, point at the down arrow located on the bottom of the vertical scrollbar.

2. Click the arrow, and the window's contents move up.

3. Click the scroll arrow on the right side of the horizontal scrollbar, and the window's contents shift to the left.

By its placement within the scrollbar, the scroll box depicts how much of a window is not visible. If you know approximately where something is in a window, you can drag the scroll box to get there quickly. To drag the scroll box and move quickly to a distant area of the window (top or bottom, left or right), use this technique:

1. Point to the scroll box in the scrollbar and press and hold the left mouse button.

2. Drag the scroll box to the new location.

3. Release the mouse button.

However, sometimes you may need to move slowly through a window (to scan for a particular icon, for example). You can move through the contents of a window one screenful at a time by clicking inside the scrollbar on either side of the scroll box.

 Empty Window?   Don't worry if text, graphics, or icons don't appear in a window. Use the scrollbar to bring them into view. Items in any window appear first in the upper-left corner.

MOVING A WINDOW

When you start working with multiple windows, moving a window becomes as important as resizing one. For example, you may need to move one or more windows to make room for other work on your desktop, or you may need to move one window to see another window's contents. You can move a window with the mouse or keyboard.

 Don't Lose the Title Bar   Be very careful that you do not move a window so far off the screen that you cannot see the title bar. If you lose the title bar, you will need to maximize the window to see the tilte bar again.

To move a window using the mouse, point at the window's title bar, press and hold the left mouse button, and drag it to a new location.

VIEWING A WINDOW'S CONTENTS

Windows NT can display the contents of a window in icon form; for example, the elements in the My Computer window are represented by pictures of a hard drive, floppy drive, and folders. Other windows, such as your hard drive window, display elements as folders and files.

You can display the contents of any window in various ways so you can better see the contents. The default, or standard, view in most windows is Large Icons (refer to Figure 2.3). Large icons help you quickly identify the contents. You also can view the contents of a window as follows:

Small Icons   Contents are displayed with a small icon next to the file or folder name; small icons represent the application in which a file was created.

List   Similar to Small Icons but the icons are even smaller than in Small Icon view.

Details   Lists icon, file or folder name, file size, file type, and last date modified. When in Details view, you can click the heading button—Name, Size, Type, or Modified—to automatically sort the contents by that heading. For example, click Name and folders appear in alphabetical order, and the filenames are listed alphabetically.

Figure 2.4 shows four windows, each with a different view of the window's contents: Large Icons, Small Icons, Details, and List.

FIGURE 2.4 Display the contents of a window in a different view so you can easily identify files or folders.

To change views of the window's contents, choose View, and then select Large Icons, Small Icons, List, or Details.

CLOSING A WINDOW

When you're finished working with a window, you should close it. This often helps speed up Windows, conserve computer memory, and keep your desktop from becoming cluttered.

To close a window, follow these steps:

1. Click the Control menu button to display the Control menu.

2. Click the Close command to close the window.

 Quickie Close To quickly close a window, double-click the Control menu button.

If you'd rather use the keyboard, select the window you want to close by clicking on it to highlight the title bar, and then press Alt+F4.

Finally, you can also close a window by clicking the Close button in the window's title bar.

In this lesson, you learned how to move, resize, and close windows. In the next lesson, you'll learn how to use menus.

3 LESSON

USING MENUS

In this lesson, you'll learn how to use toolbar buttons, select menus, open menus, choose menu commands, and use menu shortcuts.

USING TOOLBAR BUTTONS

Most windows and applications offer a toolbar containing various buttons you can use as shortcuts. Toolbar buttons represent common commands you often use in Windows, such as Cut, Copy, Undo, and so on. The tools that are available to you depend on the window or application you're using. Figure 3.1 shows the toolbar for the My Computer window.

FIGURE 3.1 Use tool buttons to speed up your work.

Handy Helpers Most Windows applications provide ToolTips, helpful descriptors of the tools on a toolbar. Position the mouse pointer over any tool button and wait a second or two. A small box containing the button's name or a description of its function appears, so you can decide whether to use the button or not.

To use a tool button, click it. Just like commands, any of a variety of results may occur. If, for example, you select a folder or file and choose the Copy tool button, a duplicate of the folder or file moves to the Windows Clipboard (described in Lesson 4, "Using dialog Boxes") for pasting to another area later. If you choose the Undo tool button, the last action you performed is reversed.

WHAT IS A MENU?

A *menu* is a list of commands that you use to perform tasks in Windows NT and in Windows applications (tasks such as copying or deleting selected items in a window). Menu commands are organized in logical groups. For example, all the commands related to arranging and opening windows are located on the Windows menu. The names of the available menus appear below the title bar of any window or application that uses menus.

Lost? Any time you're not sure what to do next or how to perform a specific task, click each menu in the application and read each command. Generally, you can find what you want this way; if not, you can always choose the Help menu (described in Lesson 5, "Using Windows NT Help").

This book uses the format *menu title, menu command* to tell you to choose a command from a pull-down menu. For example, the sentence "choose File, Properties" means to "open the File menu and select the Properties command."

Pull-Down Menu   A menu that appears to "pull-down" from the menu bar. You access the menu by clicking its name in the menu bar. You then have several options to choose from within the pull-down menu.

Choosing Menu Commands

To choose a menu command, follow these steps:

1. Click the menu title in the menu bar. The menu opens to display the available commands.

2. To choose a particular command, click it. For example, to see the View commands available for the My Computer window, click the View menu in the menu bar. The View menu appears (see Figure 3.2).

Click here to
display the menu

Figure 3.2   Click any menu title to view its contents.

3. To make the menu disappear, click anywhere outside the menu.

To choose a command on the menu, move the mouse to that command and click. What happens next depends on the menu and command.

CHOOSING MENU COMMANDS USING THE KEYBOARD

You can also select menus and menu commands with the keyboard. To do so, press Alt to activate the menu bar of the active window. The first menu title is automatically highlighted, indicating that its menu bar is active. With the menu bar active, you can select a menu using either of these two methods:

- Use the arrow keys to highlight the menu title you want, and then press Enter or the down arrow.

- Press the key that corresponds to the underlined letter of the menu. For example, to open the Help menu, press H.

After you open the menu, you select a command from the menu using the same techniques you used to open the menu. Highlight the command using the arrow keys and press Enter, or press the key that corresponds to the underlined letter to select the command you want.

To open the Control menu with the keyboard, press Alt+Spacebar in an application window (such as Microsoft Word), or press Alt+- (hyphen) in a document. Then highlight your selection using the arrow keys and press Enter, or press the key that corresponds to the underlined letter of the command. To close the Control menu (or any menu for that matter), press Esc once to hide the menu and a second time to deselect the menu bar.

Commands, Options, or Selections? Commands, menu options, and menu selections all refer to the same thing—items you choose from a menu.

READING A MENU

Windows menus contain a number of common elements that indicate what will happen when you choose a command, provide a shortcut, or limit your choice of commands. Some menus, for instance, may contain commands that are *dimmed* or grayed-out. However, most commands perform some sort of task when you select them.

Unavailable Commands If a command appears grayed-out, you cannot currently use that command. Grayed-out commands are available for use only under certain circumstances. For example, you cannot choose the Copy command or the Delete command if you have not first selected an object to copy or delete.

Depending on the type of command you select, one of four things will happen:

- **An action will take place.** For example, choosing File, Delete erases the selected icon or file.

- **A dialog box will appear.** Any command followed by an ellipsis (...) displays a dialog box containing related options. (See Lesson 4 for more information.)

- **A secondary menu will appear.** A command followed by an arrow displays a second (cascading) menu offering related commands.

- **A feature will be turned on.** A check mark or bullet appears to the left of the option you select on the menu, and that option remains active until you either select a different bulleted option in the same menu or deselect the checked option by clicking it a second time.

Separator Lines Commands on most menus are grouped together and divided by separator lines. When (bulleted) option commands are grouped, you can select only one option in the group at a time. When checked commands are grouped, you can choose as many or as few options as you want.

Figure 3.3 shows common menu elements: the ellipsis, the check mark, an option bullet, an arrow with cascading menu, and separator lines.

FIGURE 3.3   Indicators let you know what will happen before you select the command.

To practice using menu commands, follow these steps:

1. In the My Computer window, choose View, Toolbar. The Toolbar displays, if it was not already displayed.

2. Choose View, Options (notice the ellipsis after the Options command). A dialog box appears.

3. To cancel the dialog box, choose the Cancel button.

USING SHORTCUT KEYS INSTEAD OF MENUS

Until you become familiar with Windows NT and your various Windows applications, you'll need to use the menus to view and select commands. However, after you've worked in Windows for a while, you'll probably want to use shortcut keys for commands you use often. Shortcut keys enable you to select a command without using the menus. They generally combine the Alt, Ctrl, or Shift key with a letter key (such as W). If a shortcut key is available, it is listed on the pull-down menu to the right of the command.

For example, Figure 3.4 shows the Edit menu from the hard drive window on My Computer. As you can see, the shortcut key for Cut is Ctrl+X. You cannot use the shortcut key while the menu is open; you must either choose a command or cancel the menu. You can, however, remember the shortcut key and use it instead of opening the menu the next time you need to use the Cut command.

FIGURE 3.4   Use shortcut keys to save time.

USING SHORTCUT MENUS

Windows NT supplies a variety of shortcut menus that contain common commands you often use. You can display a shortcut menu by right-clicking an object—the desktop, a window, a folder or file, and so on. The commands a shortcut menu displays depends on the item and its location.

To display and use a shortcut menu, point the mouse to the object you want to explore, open, cut, copy, or otherwise manipulate, and right-click the mouse. The shortcut menu appears; move the mouse to the command and click again. Cancel a shortcut menu by clicking the mouse anywhere besides on the menu.

Figure 3.5 displays a shortcut menu resulting from right-clicking a hard drive icon.

FIGURE 3.5   Quickly access a command with a right-click.

In this lesson, you learned how to use toolbar buttons, open and read a menu, and use shortcuts. In the next lesson, you'll learn to use dialog boxes and all their components.

USING DIALOG BOXES

In this lesson, you'll learn how to use the various dialog box components.

WHAT IS A DIALOG BOX?

Windows NT and Windows applications use *dialog boxes* to exchange information with you. As you learned in Lesson 3, a menu command followed by an ellipsis (...) indicates that a dialog box will appear. A dialog box asks for information the program needs in order to complete the operation.

 What are Property Sheets?   Windows NT also uses the term *property sheets* to describe a type of dialog box. A property sheet generally presents information—such as free space on a hard drive, file attributes, and so on—about a selected element in Windows. Property sheets supply information and often offer options, just like dialog boxes.

Windows NT also displays dialog boxes to give you information. For example, Windows NT might display a dialog box to warn you about a problem (as in "File already exists, Overwrite?") or to confirm that an operation should take place (to confirm that you want to delete a file, for example).

Box Won't Go Away?   If a dialog box won't go away and your computer beeps at you when you try to continue your work, don't worry. That beep is Windows' way of telling you that you must always respond to a dialog box before you can continue. You can press Enter or choose OK to accept the message or changes in the dialog box, or you can press the Esc key or choose Cancel to cancel the message or the changes in the box.

Using the Components of a Dialog Box

Dialog boxes vary in complexity depending on the program, the procedure, and the number of options in the actual box. Some simply ask you to confirm an operation before it is executed; others ask you to choose, for example, a drive, folder, filename, file type, network path, or numerous other options.

The following list briefly explains the components of a dialog box. Not all dialog boxes contain all components, so don't be afraid to tackle a dialog box.

Text box   A text box provides a place to type an entry, such as a filename, path (drive and directory), font, or measurement.

List box   A list box presents a slate of possible options from which you can choose. Scrollbars often accompany a list box so you can view the items on the list. In addition, a text box is sometimes associated with a list box; you can either choose from the list or type the selection yourself.

Drop-down list box (also called a combo box)   This box is a single-line list box with a drop-down arrow button to the right of it. When you click the arrow, the drop-down list box opens to display a list of choices. You can often scroll through a drop-down list as you do a list box.

Option buttons   Option buttons present a group of related choices from which you can choose only one. Click the option button you want to select, and all others become deselected.

Check box   A check box enables you to turn an option on or off. You might find a single check box or a group of related check boxes. A check mark appears in the box next to any option that is active (turned on). In a group of check boxes, you can choose none, one, or any number of the options.

Command button   When selected, a command button carries out the command displayed on the button (Open, Help, Quit, Cancel, or OK, for example). If there is an ellipsis on the button (as in Option...), choosing it will open another dialog box.

Tabs   Tabs represent multiple sections, or pages, of a dialog box. Only one tab is displayed at a time, and each tab contains related options. Choosing a tab changes the options that appear in the dialog box.

USING TEXT BOXES

You use a text box to enter the information that Windows NT or a Windows application needs in order to complete a command. This information is usually a filename or folder name. Figure 4.1 shows a text box and list boxes in the Open dialog box (accessed from the Windows WordPad File menu).

To activate a text box using the mouse, position the mouse over the text box (the mouse pointer changes to an I-beam) and click. The I-beam pointer shape indicates that the area you're pointing to will accept text. Look for the I-beam when you want to enter text in a dialog box. Notice that the insertion point (a flashing vertical line) appears in the active text box.

List box

Drop-down list box

Text box

FIGURE 4.1   Use text boxes and list boxes to specify your preferences.

Save Time   If you want to replace text that's already in a text box, drag your mouse over the text (to highlight text) and start typing. When you type the first character, the original text is deleted.

To activate a text box using the keyboard, press Alt+*selection letter* (The *selection letter* is the underlined letter in a menu, command, or option name.) For example, to activate the File Name text box shown in Figure 4.1, press Alt+N. After you have activated a text box and typed text into it, you can use several keys to edit the text. Table 4.1 outlines these keys.

TABLE 4.1   EDITING KEYS FOR TEXT BOXES AND OTHER TEXT

KEY	DESCRIPTION
Delete	Deletes the character to the right of the insertion point
Backspace	Erases the character to the left of the insertion point
End	Moves the insertion point to the end of the line

continues

TABLE 4.1 CONTINUED

KEY	DESCRIPTION
Home	Moves the insertion point to the beginning of the line
Arrow keys	Moves the insertion point one character in the direction of the arrow
Shift+End	Selects the text from the insertion point to the end of the line
Shift+Home	Selects the text from the insertion point to the beginning of the line
Shift+Arrow key	Selects the next character in the direction of the arrow
Ctrl+C	Copies selected text to the Clipboard
Ctrl+V	Pastes selected text from the Clipboard

Clipboard   The Clipboard is a tool provided by Windows NT that holds any cut or copied text for you so you can paste it into another location, document, or application. For more information, see Lesson 9, "Copying and Moving Information Between Windows".

USING LIST BOXES

You use a list box to select from multiple available options. For example, you use the Look In list box in the Open dialog box (see Figure 4.1) to select the drive that contains the file you want to open.

To select an item from a list box using the mouse, click the appropriate list item and click OK (or double-click the item to be selected). You can also select more than one item in many list boxes by holding the Shift key as you click. In the Files of Type list box, notice that the item you select automatically appears in the linked text box above the list box.

To select an item from a drop-down list box using the mouse, open the list box by clicking the down-arrow, and then click the appropriate list item.

USING OPTION BUTTONS

Option buttons enable you to make a single choice from a group of possible command options. For example, the Print Range options displayed in Figure 4.2 enable you to choose which pages of your document you want to print. The active option (the All option in Figure 4.2) has a filled-in radio button.

Option buttons ———

——— Active selection

FIGURE 4.2   You can choose only one option in the group.

To select an option button with the mouse, click the circle for the option you want.

USING CHECK BOXES

For options that you can select (activate) or deselect (deactivate), Windows NT and Windows applications usually provide check boxes. When a check box is selected, an X or a check mark appears in the box, indicating the associated option is active (see Figure 4.3).

To select or deselect a check box, click its box.

FIGURE 4.3   A check mark or X indicates an active, or selected, option.

USING COMMAND BUTTONS

You use command buttons to either accept or reject the changes you've made in a dialog box, to get help, or to access another related dialog box. To select a command button with the mouse, click it.

Figure 4.4 shows the two most common command buttons: OK and Cancel. Select the OK command button to accept the information you have entered or to verify an action and close the dialog box. Select the Cancel command button to leave the dialog box without putting into effect the changes you made in the dialog box.

Shortcuts   You can press the Enter key in a dialog box to quickly accept the changes you've made and close the dialog box; similarly, you can press the Esc key to cancel the changes made to a dialog box and to close that box.

Command buttons

FIGURE 4.4   Use command buttons to control the dialog box.

You can choose the Network command button (found in many of Windows NT's dialog boxes) to access a network to which you're attached. You can access files, folders, and printers from the network or save files to network drives as long as you have permission to do so. For more information, see Lesson 18, "Securing Files and Folders".

Accidents Happen   If you accidentally select the Cancel command button in a dialog box, don't worry. You can always reenter the dialog box and continue. You need to be more careful when you select OK, however, because the instructions you have entered in the dialog box will be executed.

USING PROPERTY SHEETS AND TABS

As noted previously, property sheets are similar to dialog boxes in the components they contain: check boxes, list boxes, text boxes, command buttons, and so on. Figure 4.5 shows the Taskbar Properties property sheet.

Tabs

Figure 4.5 Choose a tab that represents the options you want to change.

In a property sheet containing more than one tab, choose options within the sheet, and then choose the Apply button to accept those changes. You can then select the other tabs and make any changes you want. Once you've chosen the Apply button, however, you cannot cancel those changes using the Cancel command button. Rather, you must select the new desired options on the tab. To select a tab, click the tab with the mouse pointer.

In this lesson, you learned to use dialog boxes and their components. In the next lesson, you'll learn to use the Windows NT Help feature.

USING WINDOWS NT HELP

In this lesson, you'll learn how to get help, use the Help feature's shortcut buttons, and use the What's This? feature.

GETTING HELP IN WINDOWS NT

Windows NT offers several ways to get online help—instant onscreen help for menu commands, procedures, features, and other items. *Online help* is information that appears in its own window whenever you request it. Windows NT's Help offers three help features: Index, Find, and Contents.

The Contents feature displays a list of topics (such as Introducing Windows NT, How To, and Troubleshooting) as well as a Glossary and tips and tricks for using NT. The Index feature enables you to access specific categories of topics—such as adapters, disk configuration, naming disks, and so on. The Find feature lets you search for specific words and phrases—such as About, Checking, Mem, Printing, and so on.

 Set Up Help   The first time you choose Find in NT Help, NT runs a Setup Wizard that compiles keywords from the Help files into a database you use to find words. Follow directions within the wizard before using Find.

Context Help Most dialog boxes, including Help dialog boxes, include a Help button (a question mark in the title bar) that enables you to get help on items within the dialog box. Click the question mark and point the mouse at an area you have a question about. NT displays a box with a definition or other information relating to your question. When you're finished reading the help, click the mouse to hide the information box.

USING THE CONTENTS FEATURE

You can get help with common procedures using Help's Contents feature. The Contents feature displays the top-level groups of information covered in Help, such as How To and Commands. When you select a major group, a list of related topics appears. Figure 5.1 shows the Contents Help window.

Document represents related topics

Book represents major group

FIGURE 5.1 Choose from the listed topics for task-specific help.

Follow these steps to use Help's Contents feature:

1. Choose the Start button, and then choose Help. The Help Topics: Windows NT Help window appears; select the Contents tab if it is not already selected.

Help Tabs The last tab in the Help Topics window that you accessed is the one that appears the next time you open Help.

2. In the Contents list, double-click the book icon in front of the topic you want to view. The book opens and related topics appear either in a list of books or documents.

3. Double-click a document icon to view information about that topic (see Figure 5.2).

FIGURE 5.2 A Help window tells you what you need to know when you have trouble printing, for example.

 More Help Anytime you see a small gray button beside a word or phrase in a Help window, you can click the button to see more information related to the topic.

5. When you finish with the Help topic, you can choose one of the following buttons:

Close (X)   To close the Help window and return to the NT desktop.

Help Topics   To return to the Contents tab of the Help Topics window and select another topic.

Back   To display the previously viewed Help window.

Options   To copy, print, or otherwise set preferences for the Help windows.

USING THE INDEX FEATURE

Help's Index feature provides a list of Help topics arranged alphabetically on the Index *tab* of the Help Topics window. Either you can enter a word for which you are searching, or you can scroll through the list to find the topic. Figure 5.3 shows the Index tab of the Help Topics: Windows NT Help window.

Tab   Much like a tab on a file folder, a tab is a division that separates different options in a dialog box. Click a tab to bring it forward so you can use it.

FIGURE 5.3   Use the Index tab to find specific words and phrases in Help.

To use the Help Index, follow these steps:

1. In the Help Topics window, choose the Index tab.

2. Click in the text box and type a topic you want to know about. As you type, Windows moves to the topics beginning with the first letters you enter.

 Browse the List   You can scroll through the index list to see what other topics are available.

3. In the list of topics, select the topic you want to view and choose Display, or double-click the topic. The Help topic window appears.

4. When you're finished with the Help topic, you can choose another option, or you can close the Help window by pressing Alt+F4.

USING THE FIND FEATURE

You can search for specific words and phrases in a Help topic instead of searching for a Help topic by category. The first time you use the Find feature, however, you have to instruct Windows to create a list that contains every word from your Help files. (You have to create the word list only once.)

The Find feature is especially useful when you cannot find a particular Help topic in Help Contents or on the Index tab's list of topics.

To use the Find feature, follow these steps:

1. In the Help Topics window, choose the Find tab. If you have used Find before, skip down to the set of steps following Figure 5.4. If you haven't previously set up the Help topics, the Find Setup Wizard dialog box appears. Continue with these steps.

2. In the Wizard dialog box, choose one of the following:

Minimize Database Size   Creates a short, limited word list.

Maximize Search Capabilities   Creates a long, detailed word list.

Customize Search Capabilities   Enables you to create a shorter word list, including only the Help files you want to use. Use this option if you have limited disk space. If you select this option, choose Next, and then choose the topics you want to include.

3. Click the Finish button to create the word list.

When Windows finishes creating the word list, the Find tab contains a text box, a word list, and a topic list, as shown in Figure 5.4.

Figure 5.4   Windows now has a word list to search through.

To search for words or a phrase in a Help topic

1. Type the word or phrase you want to find in the text box at the top of the dialog box. This enters the word for which you want to search, and Windows displays forms of the word in the word list in the middle of the Find tab.

2. If you see a word that applies to your topic, select that word to narrow your search. If you do not want to narrow the search, move on to step 3.

Topic List   Instead of typing something in the text box, you can scroll through the word list and select the word you want from the list. If you want to find words similar to the words in a Help topic, click the Find Similar button.

3. Click one or more topics in the topic list, and then click the Display button. Windows NT displays the selected Help topic information in a Windows Help window.

4. When you finish with the Help topic, you can close the Help window by pressing Alt+F4. (If, however, you want to select another option for more information, look at the next section, "Using Help Windows.")

Accidents Happen   If you don't want to use the first list that Windows creates, you're not stuck with it. You can rebuild the list to include more words or to exclude words. Click the Rebuild button and choose a word list option to recreate the word list.

USING HELP WINDOWS

When you access a Windows Help topic window, a toolbar appears at the top of the Help window and remains visible. This toolbar includes three buttons: Help Topics, Back, and Options. Table 5.1 describes each button in the toolbar of a Windows Help window as well as the Options menu.

TABLE 5.1   WINDOWS HELP TOOLBAR BUTTONS AND MENU

BUTTON	DESCRIPTION
Help Topics	Opens the Help Topics: Windows NT Help window containing the Contents, Index, and Find tabs
Back	Displays the previous Help topic window you viewed during the current session
Options	Displays a menu containing the following commands: Annotate, Copy, Print Topic, Font, Keep Help on Top, and Use System Colors

The following list describes the Options menu commands in more detail:

Annotate   Enables you to mark any text or topic in a Help window so you can easily find the topic later. A Paper Clip icon appears beside any annotated text in Help.

Copy   Place a copy of the text in a Help window on the Windows Clipboard (described in Lesson 9, "Copying and Moving Information Between Windows") for pasting to another document, application, or window.

Print Topic   Send the text in the Help window to the printer for a hard copy.

Font   Select from Small, Normal, or Large type to view the help text. Normal is the default.

Keep Help on Top   Choose whether to always display the Help window on top of all documents and windows so you can easily follow directions as you work.

Use System Colors   Choose this option to restart the Help feature and change the colors in the Help box.

USING THE WHAT'S THIS? FEATURE

The *What's This?* feature provides a handy way for you to get more information about dialog box options. You activate this feature by selecting the ? icon that appears at the right end of the title bar in some (but not all) Windows NT dialog boxes. Figure 5.5 shows a window with the What's This? icon and a description you might see if you clicked that icon.

Description —

FIGURE 5.5   Use the What's This? feature to get help on certain dialog box elements.

The following steps tell you how to use the What's This? feature to display a description of any option in a Windows NT dialog box offering the What's This? feature.

1. Click the ? icon in the upper-right corner of the Windows NT dialog box. A large question mark appears next to the mouse pointer.

2. Click any option in the dialog box, and Windows NT displays a box containing a short description of the item you selected.

3. When you finish reading the Help information, click anywhere on the screen to close the Help box.

 Quick Description   If you right-click an option in the dialog box, a shortcut menu appears displaying one menu command: What's This? Click What's This? to view a description of the option. Note, however, that this works only if the dialog box contains a question mark in its title bar.

In this lesson, you learned how to access and use the features in Windows NT's Help system. In the next lesson, you'll learn how to start and exit applications.

STARTING AND EXITING APPLICATIONS IN WINDOWS NT

In this lesson, you'll learn how to start and exit an NT application as well as how to view the common elements of application windows.

OPENING AN NT APPLICATION

Windows NT 4 provides a Start menu from which you can perform many tasks, including starting Windows programs. To display the Start menu, click the Start button on the Windows taskbar. You can open the Help feature from the Start menu; you also can open various applications from the Start menu by choosing the Programs command. The menus you see stemming from the Programs menu will vary depending on your system setup (see Figure 6.1).

To open an application, follow these steps:

1. Choose the Start button.

2. Select Programs to display the Programs menu.

3. Choose the application you want to open, if it's listed on the Programs menu; alternatively, select the group containing the application you want to open.

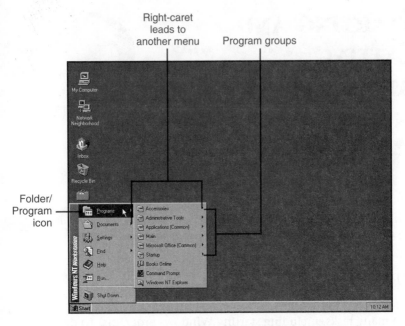

Figure 6.1   Access applications from the Programs menu.

Program Groups   The Programs menu displays various group names—such as Accessories, Administrative Tools, Applications, and so on—that display a menu of related applications when selected. You can identify a program group by the Folder/Program icon in front of it and the right-arrow following the command. Accessories and Administrative Tools are programs installed when you install NT. You may also have program groups for Microsoft Office, Lotus SmartSuite, or other applications you've installed on your computer.

Open Documents   If you have a specific document you have recently worked on and want to open, you can click the Documents command on the Start menu to display a list; click the document you want to open and the source application opens with the document, ready for you to work on.

VIEWING AN APPLICATION'S SCREEN

Depending on the application you open—whether it's a word processor, database, spreadsheet, or other program—the screen will include elements particular to the tasks and procedures used for that application. For example, the mouse may appear as an I-beam, an arrow, or a cross; the document area may appear as a blank sheet of paper or a table with many cells.

Most applications, however, display the following elements: title bar, menu bar, toolbars, ruler, scrollbars, a document area, and a status bar. Figure 6.2 shows the screen you see when you open Microsoft Word.

 Get Help   If you need help with any application, you can click the Help menu and select a Help topic.

FIGURE 6.2   Most application screens contain similar elements.

EXITING AN APPLICATION

You should always exit an application when you're done with it to ensure that your documents are saved before shutting Windows down. You can exit most Windows NT applications in one of the following ways:

- Choose the File menu, and then select the Exit command.

- Click the Close button (X), located in the upper-right corner of the title bar.

- Choose Close from the Control menu, located in the upper-left corner of the title bar.

- Double-click the application's Control menu icon.

- Press Alt+F4.

Message Before Closing?   If the application displays a message asking if you want to save the document before you close the program, choose Yes to save, or choose No to close the application without saving the changes. Choose Cancel to return to the application. If you choose Yes, the application displays the Save As dialog box in which you assign the document a name and location on your computer.

In this lesson, you learned to open and exit a Windows NT application and to view the common elements of application windows. In the next lesson, you'll learn to shut down Windows NT.

7

SHUTTING DOWN WINDOWS NT

In this lesson, you'll learn to log off the network and to shut down Windows NT.

LOGGING OFF

You log off Windows NT Workstation anytime you want to restart the computer. In addition, you might need to log off so you can log on using another user account. For example, if you're a member of two or more groups, you might have different access permissions for various resources. Additionally, if more than one person has access to your computer, you log off so another can log on. Therefore, you might have to log off and log back on using another account in order to continue your work.

To log off, follow these steps:

1. Press Ctrl+Alt+Del. The Windows NT Security dialog box appears. In the Logon Information, NT lists who you are, as well as the logon date.

2. Click the Logoff command button to log off the network. The Logoff Windows NT dialog box appears.

3. Click OK. Press Ctrl+Alt+Del to log on as a different user.

As an alternative to displaying the Windows NT Security dialog box, you can log off by choosing Start, Shut Down, and then choosing the Close All Programs and Log On As a Different User option. Choose Yes to confirm your choice. Press Ctrl+Alt+Del to open the Log On dialog box, in which you enter the username and password you want to use to log on to Windows NT.

Ctrl+Alt+Del   In MS-DOS, this key combination warm boots your computer. In Windows NT, however, pressing this key combination when you first start the operating system displays the Password dialog box. If you press Ctrl+Alt+Del when you're already in the program, you see the Windows NT Security dialog box instead.

As you may have noticed, the Windows NT Security dialog box contains a number of other useful command buttons:

Lock Workstation   Secures your computer so no one else can access it while you're away from your desk.

Change Password   Displays the Change Password dialog box, where you can enter a new password for logging on to your computer.

Task Manager   Displays the Task List, which you can use to cancel or end an application that is not responding.

Shutdown   Displays the Shutdown Computer dialog box, in which you can choose to either Shutdown or Shutdown and Restart.

Cancel   Cancels the dialog box and returns you to the Program Manager.

SHUTTING DOWN THE COMPUTER

You shut down Windows NT when you want to turn your computer off.

Don't Touch that Power Switch   Never turn off your computer with the power switch until after you have shut down Windows NT. If you do, you may lose valuable data.

To shut down Windows NT, follow these steps:

1. From the desktop, choose Start, Shut Down.

2. When the Shutdown Windows dialog box appears, choose Shut Down the Computer, and then choose Yes.

3. Do not turn the computer off until Windows NT displays a message telling you that it is okay to turn off your computer.

 Alternative Shutdown   You can also press Ctrl+Alt+Del and choose the Shutdown button from the Windows NT Security dialog box.

In this lesson, you learned to log off the network and to shut down Windows NT. In the next lesson, you'll learn to work with multiple windows onxscreen at one time.

WORKING WITH MULTIPLE WINDOWS

In this lesson, you'll learn how to arrange windows, switch between windows in the same application, and switch between applications.

In Windows NT, you can use more than one application at a time, and in each Windows application, you can work with multiple document windows. As you can imagine, opening multiple applications with multiple windows can make your desktop pretty cluttered. That's why it's important that you know how to manipulate and switch between windows. The following sections explain how to do that.

ARRANGING WINDOWS ON THE DESKTOP

When you have multiple windows open, some windows or parts of windows are inevitably hidden by others, which makes the screen confusing. You can use various commands to arrange your open windows. To access the cascade and tile windows commands, right-click the mouse in any open area of the taskbar, and then select the command from the shortcut menu.

 Quick! Clean the Desktop You can minimize all windows by choosing one command to quickly clear the desktop of open windows. Right-click the taskbar and choose Minimize All Windows. All open windows then become buttons on the taskbar.

CASCADING WINDOWS

A good way to get a clear view of a confusing desktop is to open
the Taskbar Shortcut menu and choose the Cascade command.
When you choose this command, Windows lays all the open windows on top of each other so that the title bar of each is visible.
Figure 8.1 shows a cascaded window arrangement using WordPad,
Solitaire, and Chat. To access any window that's not on the top,
click its title bar. That window then becomes the *active window*.

Active Window   The active window is the one in which
you are working. You activate a window by clicking its
title bar or anywhere inside the window, or by clicking
its button on the taskbar. The active window's title bar
becomes highlighted, and if the windows are cascaded,
the active window comes to the front.

Other open
windows

Active
window

FIGURE 8.1   With cascaded windows, you can easily access the
one you need.

You can still click and drag the title bar of any window to another location on the desktop and you can use the mouse to resize the window borders of any open window.

TILING WINDOWS

If you need to see all open windows at the same time, open the Taskbar shortcut menu and select either the Tile Horizontally or Tile Vertically command. When you choose to Tile, Windows resizes and moves each open window so that they all appear side by side (vertically) or one on top of the other (horizontally), as shown in Figure 8.2.

FIGURE 8.2   Tile windows so you can see a part of each window at the same time without overlap.

MOVING BETWEEN APPLICATIONS

Windows NT enables you to have multiple applications open at the same time. If the open application windows are not maximized, you might be able to see all those open windows overlapped, onscreen. In this case you can click any window to bring it forward. Often, however, it's easier to work in a single application by maximizing the application's window. Switching between applications then requires a different procedure. You'll most likely use the taskbar to switch from application to application by clicking the minimized application button on the taskbar.

After opening several applications—such as WordPad, Paint, and the Chat feature, for example—you can use the taskbar by following these steps:

1. On the taskbar, click the button representing the application you want to open (see Figure 8.3).

2. To switch to another open application, click its button on the taskbar. The open window minimizes back to the taskbar and is replaced by the next application you select.

FIGURE 8.3   All open and minimized applications appear on the taskbar.

MOVING BETWEEN WINDOWS IN THE SAME APPLICATION

In addition to working in multiple applications in Windows NT, you can also open multiple windows within an application. Moving to a new window means you are changing the window that is active. If you are using a mouse, you can move to a window by clicking any part of it. When you do, the title bar becomes highlighted, and that particular window comes to the front so you can work in it.

Figure 8.4 shows multiple document windows open in Microsoft Word. You can switch between the windows, arrange windows, and open and close windows.

FIGURE 8.4   Three document windows are open within the program.

Open multiple document windows using the File, Open command. By default, each window is maximized within the document area. To switch between open, maximized windows, click the Window menu and select the document from the list at the bottom of the menu. Alternatively, you can press Ctrl+F6 to cycle through the open windows.

To view multiple document windows onscreen, follow these steps:

1. Restore the document window by clicking the document's Restore button. The open document windows cascade in the document area. The Restore button replaces the Maximize button.

2. To activate an open document window, click in the window's title bar or press Ctrl+F6.

3. To tile all the windows, choose Window, Arrange All. Windows reduces each open document window and tiles them (horizontally) in the document area.

They're All Just Windows You can use the window frames to resize each window. Likewise, you can minimize, maximize, open, and close the windows as you would any window. (See Lesson 2, "Working with a Window" for instructions.)

In this lesson, you learned to arrange open windows, switch between application windows, and switch document windows within an application. In the next lesson, you'll learn to copy and move information between windows.

COPYING AND MOVING INFORMATION BETWEEN WINDOWS

In this lesson, you'll learn about the ClipBook and Clipboard and how to copy and move information between windows.

WHAT ARE THE CLIPBOOK AND THE CLIPBOARD?

One of the handiest features of the Windows NT environment is its capability to copy or move information (text, graphics, and files) from one application to another. This feature enables you to share information between document windows, applications, and other computers on the network.

Windows NT includes a *ClipBook Viewer*. The ClipBook Viewer contains a window representing your local ClipBook and the Clipboard. The *Clipboard* temporarily stores data, and the ClipBook permanently stores data that you want to save and share with others on your network.

When you *cut* or *copy* data from an application, it's placed on the Clipboard and it remains there until you cut or copy again. You can *paste* the data from the Clipboard to a document or application. Note, however, that you don't have to open the Clipboard to use it—and 95 percent of the time, you won't. You'll just cut or copy your data, and then paste it to a new location.

Copy, Cut, and Paste When you copy information, the application copies it to the Clipboard without disturbing the original. When you cut information, the application removes it from its original location and places it on the Clipboard. When you paste information, the application inserts the information that's on the Clipboard in the location you specify. (The copy on the Clipboard remains intact, so you can use it again if necessary.)

As mentioned earlier, data you copy or cut to the Clipboard remains there only until you cut or copy something else. However, you can save data that is stored in the Clipboard by copying it to your Local ClipBook and saving it as a page. At any time, you can add more cut or copied data to additional pages in the ClipBook, creating a saved page that others on the network can use. Figure 9.1 shows the ClipBook Viewer with both the Local ClipBook and the Clipboard windows open. Data that was recently copied appears in the Clipboard window. Saved data appears in the Local ClipBook window.

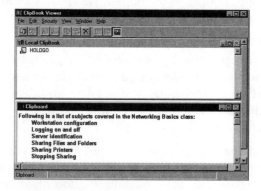

FIGURE 9.1   The ClipBook Viewer.

You can see the contents of the Local ClipBook and the Clipboard at any time by following these steps. (See the following sections in this lesson to find out how to get text into the ClipBook and the Clipboard.)

1. From the desktop, select Start, Programs, Accessories. Then choose Clipboard Viewer from the Accessories menu. The ClipBook Viewer window opens.

2. Click the Restore button in the Clipboard title bar if the window is minimized in the ClipBook Viewer window. The Clipboard window opens.

3. To close the ClipBook Viewer window, click the Close (X) button.

To save the Clipboard contents as a file, follow these steps:

1. Make the Clipboard window active, and then choose File, Save As.

2. In the File Name text box, enter a filename. You can use long filenames if you want. Then choose Save.

 Without a Trace   When you turn off your computer or exit Windows NT, the contents of the Clipboard disappear. Be sure to save any Clipboard contents you want to keep.

SELECTING TEXT FOR COPYING OR MOVING

Before you can copy or cut text, you must identify the text by selecting it. Selected text appears in reverse video (highlighted). Figure 9.2 shows selected text in a WordPad document.

To select text with the mouse

1. Position the mouse pointer just before the first character you want to select.

2. Press and hold the left mouse button, and drag the mouse pointer to the last character you want selected.

3. Release the mouse button, and the selected text is high-lighted.

FIGURE 9.2 You must select text in order to copy or cut it.

 Text Selection Shortcut To select a single word using the mouse, double-click the word.

To select text with the keyboard

1. Use the arrow keys to position the insertion point (the blinking vertical line) just before the first character you want to select.

2. Press and hold down the Shift key and use the arrow keys to move the highlight to the last character you want to select.

3. Release all keys, and the selected text appears highlighted.

To cancel any selection (deselect it), click anywhere in the document or press an arrow key.

 Where's My Selected Text? If you press an alphanumeric key (a letter, number, or any other character) while text is highlighted, Windows deletes the selected text and replaces it with the character you typed. Choose Edit, Undo, or press Ctrl+Z to reverse the action.

SELECTING GRAPHICS

The procedure for selecting graphics depends on the Windows application you are using. In a word-processing program such as Write, you select a graphic by clicking the object. In a program such as Paintbrush, however, there are special tools for copying and cutting either rectangular or irregular shapes. Because the procedure varies, you should refer to the instructions for each application.

COPYING INFORMATION BETWEEN WINDOWS

After you select text or graphics, the procedures for copying and pasting are the same in all Windows applications. To copy and paste information between windows of the same application, as well as between windows of different applications, follow these steps:

1. Select the text or graphic to copy.

2. Click the Copy button on the toolbar, or choose Edit, Copy. A copy of the selected material is placed on the Clipboard; the original selection remains in place.

3. Click to position the insertion point where you want to insert the selection. You can switch between document windows or between applications.

4. Click the Paste button or choose Edit, Paste. Windows copies the selection from the Clipboard to your document.

 Multiple Copies   Because the selected item remains on the Clipboard until you copy or cut again, you can paste information from the Clipboard multiple times.

MOVING INFORMATION BETWEEN WINDOWS

After you select text or graphics, the procedures for cutting and pasting are also the same in all Windows applications. To cut and paste information between windows of the same application or windows of different applications, follow these steps:

1. Select the text or graphic to cut.

2. Click the Cut button or choose Edit, Cut. Windows NT removes the selection from its original location and places it on the Clipboard.

3. Click to position the insertion point where you want to insert the selection. (You may need to open another application or document.)

4. Click the Paste button or choose Edit, Paste. Windows copies the selection from the Clipboard to your document. (A copy remains on the Clipboard until you cut or copy something else.)

USING THE CLIPBOOK TO SHARE DATA

You can use the ClipBook Viewer to share with others on your network the data you have saved in your ClipBook. Additionally, you can access the data in other computers' ClipBook Viewers.

SAVING DATA TO THE CLIPBOOK

Before you can share the data on your Clipboard, you must save the data to your Local ClipBook. To save data from the Clipboard to the Local ClipBook, follow these steps:

1. From the desktop, select Start, Programs, Accessories. Then choose Clipboard Viewer from the Accessories menu. The ClipBook Viewer window opens.

2. Click the Local ClipBook window to activate it.

3. Choose Edit, Paste, and the Paste dialog box appears.

4. Enter a name for the page and choose the Share Item Now check box (see Figure 9.3).

FIGURE 9.3   Create a ClipBook page to share.

5. Choose OK. An icon representing the pasted data appears in the Local ClipBook page, and the Share ClipBook Page dialog box appears.

6. In the Share ClipBook Page dialog box, choose from the following options:

   Start Application on Connect   Choose this, and your computer automatically starts the application used to create the shared data when someone tries to access the data. (The application must be running for another user to access formatted data.) You don't need to select this option if the ClipBook contains plain text or a bitmap file.

   Run Minimized   If you choose to Start Application on Connect, choose this option so you will not be bothered with the running application as you work.

7. Choose OK to close the dialog box. You can share as many pages as you want by copying the data to the Clipboard, and then following these steps to save to the ClipBook.

ACCESSING OTHER CLIPBOOK VIEWERS

You have to connect to a ClipBook on another computer in order to share that computer's ClipBook pages. To copy another computer's ClipBook pages, follow these steps:

1. In your ClipBook Viewer, choose File, Connect. The Select Computer dialog box shown in Figure 9.4 appears.

2. Either select the computer to which you want to connect from the Select Computer list, or type the computer name in the Computer text box if you don't see it in the list.

FIGURE 9.4   You connect to another computer to get ClipBook data.

   Two Backslashes?   If you type the name of the computer in the Computer text box, you must start with two backslashes.

3. Choose OK to connect to the other computer's ClipBook Viewer.

4. In the other computer's ClipBook Viewer, select the pages you want to copy and choose Edit, Copy. The pages are copied to your Clipboard.

5. Choose File, Disconnect to return to your ClipBook Viewer.

In this lesson, you learned how to copy and move information between windows and share ClipBook data with other users. In the next lesson, you'll learn how to use the Windows Explorer to manage files.

LESSON 10

VIEWING DRIVES, FOLDERS, AND FILES WITH THE WINDOWS EXPLORER

In this lesson, you'll learn how to use the Windows Explorer to view a disk's contents.

STARTING THE WINDOWS EXPLORER

You use the Explorer to organize, rename, copy, move, delete, share, and otherwise manage your folders (directories) and files. You start the Explorer from the menu. In the Start menu, choose Programs, and then choose Windows NT Explorer. The Explorer window opens.

USING THE EXPLORER WINDOW

At the top of the Explorer window, Windows NT gives the name of the drive whose contents you are currently looking at. In addition, the Explorer window is split into two panes. By default, the left pane displays your hard disk and the folders it contains. The right pane displays a list of the files stored in the selected folder. Figure 10.1 shows the Explorer window.

Drive window path   Title bar   Menu bar   Toolbar

Folder and program (left) pane   File and subfolder (right) pane   Status bar

FIGURE 10.1   Use the Explorer to manage your drives.

Table 10.1 describes the elements in the Explorer window. If you
do not see a toolbar or status bar on your screen, open the View
menu and select the item you want to display.

TABLE 10.1   EXPLORER WINDOW ELEMENTS

ELEMENT	DESCRIPTION
Title bar	Contains the window name (Exploring), the drive name, a Control menu, and the Minimize, Maximize, and Close buttons for the Explorer
Menu bar	Displays menus related to disk, folder, file, and network operations
Drive window path	Displays the current path in the window's title bar

continues

TABLE 10.1 CONTINUED

ELEMENT	DESCRIPTION
Toolbar	Provides various tools for navigating the Explorer
Folder and program pane	Displays the root directory (or drive) and any additional folders on the selected drive
File/Subfolder pane	Displays the contents of the selected folder in the folder window
Status bar	Displays such statistics as free space on drive, number of files in a folder, and so on

Subfolders A subfolder is a folder within another folder—the same thing as a subdirectory.

Folder and File Icons Each folder (directory) has a Folder icon beside it, and each file has an icon that represents its file type (such as sheets of paper, window boxes, or graphics).

To display drives, folders, and files, follow these steps:

1. In the left pane, scroll the list of drives and folders using the scrollbar. The list displays floppy drives, hard drives, CD drives, the Network Neighborhood, and so on. Select the drive you want to view by clicking it.

2. In the left pane, double-click any folder to display its additional folders in the folder pane. In the right pane, click a folder once to display its contents (files and folders).

VIEWING FOLDERS

Collapsed folders are represented by a plus sign in the folders pane of the Explorer window; expanded folders are represented by a minus sign. Figure 10.2 shows both collapsed and expanded folders.

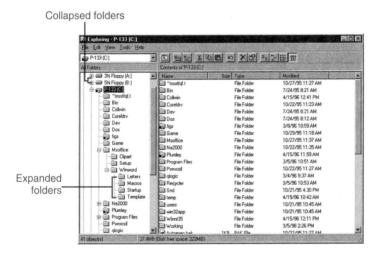

FIGURE 10.2 Expand a folder to see its contents; collapse it to hide its contents.

To expand a folder so you can view its contents, click the plus sign preceding the folder in the folders pane of the Explorer window.

To collapse a folder to hide its contents, click the minus sign preceding the folder.

Open Folders To open any folder in the right pane of the Explorer, double-click the folder and its contents appear below it in the right pane.

VIEWING AND SORTING FILES

In addition to the file name, you can view various details about the files in a folder: the date created, file type, and file size.

To view file details, choose View, Details. Windows displays the filename, type, size, and creation or modification date (see Figure 10.3).

FIGURE 10.3 You might need to see file details.

You also can use the heading buttons in the files pane to sort the files. To sort files, click one of the heading buttons shown in Figure 10.3 and described here:

Sort files by name   Alphabetically sorts files by name, A to Z on the first click and Z to A on the second click.

Sort files by type   Alphabetically sorts files by the file type (Application, Font, Help, and so on), A to Z on the first click and Z to A on the second click. Notice folders come first in the A to Z sort.

Sort files by size   Sorts files by size, largest to smallest on the first click and smallest to largest on the second click.

Sort files by date   Sorts files by date, earliest files created first on the first click and most recently created or modified first on the second click.

 Second Sort Method   You can choose the View menu, Arrange Icons command and choose to sort the files by Name, Type, Size, or Date using the secondary menu.

CLOSING THE EXPLORER

To close the Windows Explorer, choose File, Close, or click the Close (X) button.

In this lesson, you learned how to use the Windows Explorer to examine the contents of a disk. In the next lesson, you'll learn how to create and delete files and folders.

11 CREATING AND DELETING FILES AND FOLDERS

In this lesson, you'll learn how to create folders, how to delete files and folders, and how to use the Recycle Bin.

CREATING A FOLDER

Many folders are created automatically when you install a program. For example, when you install Word for Windows, the installation program creates a folder on your hard disk and places the Word for Windows files in that folder. You can use an application's designated document folders, or you can create folders yourself. For example, you might create a folder to hold any of the following groups of files:

- Subject-related files (such as all sales documents, whether they are spreadsheet, word processing, or accounting files)

- Application-related files (such as all word-processing files or, more specifically, all letters to customers)

- The files for an application that does not create its own folder during installation

- All files you'll share with other network users

To create a folder using the Explorer, follow these steps:

1. From the desktop, choose Start, Programs, and Windows NT Explorer. The Explorer window opens.

2. In the Drive Window Path on the toolbar, click the drop-down arrow. From the drop-down list, select the drive on which you want to create the new folder.

3. In the left pane, select the folder that you want to be the *parent*, or *root*, folder of your new folder.

 Root, Parent Folders   The root folder is the same as the drive. For example, C is the root folder of the hard disk. The root folder is also the parent of all folders on that drive, and any folder is the parent to all folders it contains. (Think of the parent as the drawer holding the file folders.)

4. Choose File, New, Folder, and a new folder appears in the right pane, with the name "New Folder."

5. Type a name for the new folder in the highlighted text box (see Figure 11.1).

6. Press Enter to complete the process.

FIGURE **11.1**   Add a folder to help organize your work.

Rename a Folder   To rename a folder, select the folder in the Explorer and choose File, Rename. The folder's name appears highlighted in a box; type the new name and press Enter to finish.

DELETING A FILE OR FOLDER

You should delete a file or folder when you no longer need it, when your disk is getting full, or if you created the file or folder by mistake. Before you delete anything, however, it is a good idea to make a backup copy in case you discover a need for it later; make that backup copy to a floppy disk if you're trying to save disk space. See Lesson 12, "Moving and Copying Files and Folders," for directions on how to copy files and folders.

In Windows NT, deleted items are moved to an area called the Recycle Bin and remain there until you empty the bin. Deleting items to the Recycle Bin does not provide any extra disk space. Those items remain on the disk until you empty the Recycle Bin.

To delete a file or folder, follow these steps:

1. In the Explorer, select the file or folder you want to delete by clicking it. You can select multiple files by holding the Ctrl key as you click the files you want to select.

Oops!   If you delete a parent folder, Windows NT deletes everything in it as well. Be careful to delete only those files and folders you no longer need!

2. Choose File, Delete or press the Delete key. The Delete dialog box appears, asking you to confirm that you want to delete the specified item (see Figure 11.2).

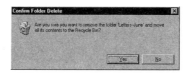

FIGURE 11.2   Delete unwanted files or folders.

3. Select Yes, and Windows NT moves the item to the Re-
    cycle Bin.

USING THE RECYCLE BIN

The Window NT Recycle Bin holds deleted files and folders until
you empty the bin or recover the files. You can open the Recycle
Bin at any time to view the items in it.

EMPTYING THE BIN

You can empty the Recycle Bin from the Explorer or from the
desktop. You should check the Bin's contents before you empty it
to be sure you're not deleting something you really want to save.
You can view the Bin from the Explorer.

To view and then empty the Recycle Bin, follow these steps:

1. In the Explorer, scroll to the bottom of the left pane until
    you see the Recycle Bin.

2. Double-click the Recycle Bin to display its contents in the
    right pane (see Figure 11.3).

3. To empty the Bin, choose File, Empty Recycle Bin. NT
    displays a Confirmation dialog box.

4. Choose Yes to delete the files.

Deleted Files   Once you empty the Recycle Bin, those
files and folders are deleted and cannot be retrieved.

FIGURE 11.3   View the bin's contents in the Explorer.

RECOVERING DELETED FILES FROM THE BIN

You can move files and folders to the Recycle Bin and then change your mind before deleting them completely from the disk. When you recover a file or folder from the bin, you're moving it back to its original drive and folder.

To recover files in the Recycle Bin, follow these steps:

1. In the Explorer, open the Recycle Bin so you can view the files and folders it contains.

2. Select any files or folders you want to recover and choose File, Restore. NT moves the selected files and folders back to their original place on your hard drive.

In this lesson, you learned how to create folders and delete files and folders. In the next lesson, you'll learn how to move and copy files and folders.

MOVING AND COPYING FILES AND FOLDERS

12

In this lesson, you'll learn how to select multiple files and folders and how to copy and move them.

SELECTING MULTIPLE FILES OR FOLDERS

To speed up operations, you can select multiple files or folders and then perform an action—such as copying, moving, deleting, or printing—on the entire group. For example, you may want to select several files to copy to a disk. Copying them all at once is much faster than copying each file individually. You select multiple files and folders in one of two ways, depending on whether they are *contiguous* or *noncontiguous* in the Windows Explorer window.

 Contiguous Contiguous files are ones that are located next to each other.

SELECTING MULTIPLE CONTIGUOUS FILES OR FOLDERS

To select contiguous files or folders with the mouse, follow these steps:

1. In the Explorer, click the first file or folder you want to select, and it becomes highlighted.

It's Not Working!   You cannot select multiple folders in the left pane; you can select multiple folders listed only in the right pane.

2. Hold down the Shift key and click the last file or folder that you want to select. Windows highlights all the items between (and including) the first and last selections. Figure 12.1 shows a selection of contiguous files.

3. To deselect all selected items with the mouse, click any one file or folder. To deselect only one or two items, continue to hold the Shift key, and then click the selected items you want to deselect.

Selected files   Selected folders

FIGURE 12.1   Select two or more contiguous files or folders by holding the Shift key and clicking the files with the mouse.

SELECTING NONCONTIGUOUS FILES OR FOLDERS

Often, the files or folders you want to select are noncontiguous—separated by one or more files between them. To select noncontiguous files or folders, use the Ctrl key.

To select noncontiguous files or folders with the mouse, follow
these steps:

1. Select the first file or folder.

2. Hold down the Ctrl key and click the other files or folders
   you want to select. Each item you click becomes highlighted and remains highlighted unless and until you
   deselect the items. Release the Ctrl key when you've completed your selections. Figure 12.2 shows a selection of
   multiple noncontiguous files.

FIGURE 12.2   Select files that are not in sequence by holding the
Ctrl key when you click.

3. To deselect all selected items with the mouse, click
   any one file or folder. To deselect only one or two items,
   continue to hold the Ctrl key, and then click the selected
   items to deselect them.

Selecting All Files   If you want to select all the files in the right pane of the Explorer, press Ctrl+A or choose Edit, Select All.

MOVING OR COPYING FILES OR FOLDERS

The time will come when you will want to rearrange files and folders on your system. For example, you might need to move a file from a folder of word processing files to a folder of files related to a particular subject. Or, you might want to copy files you've created into a folder to which certain other users have access. Windows NT provides you with two methods for doing this: menu commands and drag and drop.

Before you begin moving or copying files, take these warnings into consideration:

- When you copy or move a folder, you also copy or move the files and other folders within the folder.

- If you move application files to another folder, you may have trouble starting the applications through the Start, Programs menu. Your best bet is to leave application files in their original locations.

USING DRAG AND DROP

The easiest way to move or copy files and folders to a new location in the Explorer is to use drag and drop. To drag and drop, you select the items you want from your source folder, hold down the mouse button, move the mouse to the destination folder, and release the mouse button.

To use the drag-and-drop method of copying or moving files, follow these steps:

1. In the right pane, display the folder or file you want to move or copy.

2. Select the files you want to copy or move.

3. To copy the files, point to any of the selected files, press and hold the Ctrl key, press the mouse button, and drag the files to the folder or drive icon where you want the copy placed.

4. To move the files, point to any of the selected files, press the mouse button, and then drag the files to the folder or drive icon to which you want to move the files.

 Confirm File Replacement   If you attempt to copy a file or folder to a location in which a file or folder with the same name exists, Windows NT lets you know with a message that displays the selected file's and the original file's size and creation or last modification date. Click Yes to replace the file, or click No to stop the process.

USING THE MENUS

You can use the Copy and Cut commands on the Edit menu. To use the menus to copy or move selected file(s) or folders, follow these steps:

1. Select the files or folders you want to move or copy.

2. Open the Edit menu and select Cut or Copy. The selected items are either moved or copied to the Clipboard described in Lesson 9, "Copying and Moving Information Between Windows".

3. In the left pane of the Explorer, select the drive or folder to which you want to move or copy the selected files or folders.

4. Choose the Edit, Paste. Windows moves or copies the selected file(s) or folder(s) to the new location.

In this lesson, you learned to select multiple files and folders and to copy and move files and folders. In the next lesson, you'll learn how to rename and find files and folders.

13 RENAMING AND FINDING FILES AND FOLDERS

In this lesson, you'll learn how to rename files and folders and how to find files and folders.

RENAMING FILES AND FOLDERS

You might rename a file or folder to reorganize or to update your work; you might rename files to convert from the old eight-character names to longer, more descriptive ones. The more files and folders you create and use, the more likely it is that you will need to rename them.

To rename a file or folder, follow these steps:

1. In the Windows Explorer, select the file or folder you want to rename.

2. Choose File, Rename. The current name becomes highlighted and appears in a box with the mouse I-beam, as shown in Figure 13.1.

3. Enter the new name for the file or folder.

4. Press Enter. The new name appears beside the file or folder's icon.

 But It Worked Yesterday! Never rename program files (most have extensions EXE, COM, PIF, or BAT). Many applications will not work if their files have been renamed. Also, don't rename any files with the INI, DAT, or DLL extensions.

FIGURE 13.1   You can change the name of a file or folder.

SEARCHING FOR A FILE

The Windows NT Find program (Start menu, Find, Files or Folders) works similarly to the Explorer's search program. To search for a file, follow these steps:

1. From the Windows Explorer, choose Tools, Find, Files or Folders. The Find dialog box appears with the Name & Location tab open (see Figure 13.2).

2. In the Named text box, type the name of the file or folder you want to find (use *wildcards* in place of unknown characters).

FIGURE 13.2   Tell Windows what to search for and where to begin the search.

Wildcard A character that fills in for other character(s). When you're not sure of the filename you want to find, you can use the asterisk wildcard (*) to replace multiple characters in the actual name, such as *DOC. You can also use the question mark wildcard (?) to replace one character in the filename, such as proj04??.doc.

3. In the Look In text box, enter the drive or folders you want to search. If you enter **C:**, for example, Windows NT searches all drive C. You can, alternatively, choose the Browse button to select the drive or folder you want to search.

Include Subfolders Make sure this option is checked so Windows NT searches all subfolders within the folders you've specified for the search.

4. Choose Find Now, and Windows NT searches for the files that meet your criteria. When it finishes the search, you see the results at the bottom of the Find dialog box. Figure 13.3 shows the results of the search C:*.DOC. Notice that the title bar of the Find dialog box includes the search criteria.

5. When you finish checking out the results, close the Find dialog box.

FIGURE 13.3   The results of the search for DOC files.

In this lesson, you learned how to rename a file or folder and how to search for a file or folder. In the next lesson, you'll learn to work with Windows fonts.

LESSON 14

WORKING WITH WINDOWS FONTS

In this lesson, you'll learn how to find out which fonts you have, add new fonts, and delete the fonts you no longer need.

FINDING OUT WHICH FONTS YOU HAVE

A *font* is the typeface and style of the type you use in your documents. Some fonts that are available in most Windows applications are Times New Roman, Courier, and Arial. Windows NT supports *TrueType* fonts.

 TrueType Fonts   Fonts that are scalable (easily resized) and that look the same in your printed document as they look onscreen. TrueType fonts come with Windows NT and can be used in any of your Windows programs.

In addition to the fonts that come with Windows NT, you may also want to use *printer fonts* that come with your printer software or on cartridges you insert into your printer, or you may want to add fonts from a disk or CD-ROM that you purchase from a third-party dealer. Printer fonts may not look the same onscreen as they do when you print your documents.

Bitmapped Fonts   Windows supports fonts other than TrueType fonts. Bitmapped fonts store a unique bitmap (or graphic) image for each font in each size. Bitmapped fonts are formed by small dots, or pixels, whereas TrueType fonts are created from an outline.

The Fonts window (shown in Figure 14.1) contains a list of fonts available on your system. You also can use this window to install fonts to and remove them from your system.

Figure 14.1   Use the Fonts window to view the fonts that are on your system.

To open the window, follow these steps:

1. From the desktop, open the Start menu and choose Settings; select the Control Panel. In the Control Panel window, double-click the Fonts folder icon. The Fonts window appears.

2. Scroll through the Installed Fonts list box to see which fonts are installed on your system.

View Window's Contents You can change the view of the window's contents by choosing the View menu and selecting Large Icons, List, List Fonts by Similarity, or Details. You also can choose the Hide Variations command from the View menu to hide the bold and italic fonts listings.

3. To view a sample of any of the fonts in the list, double-click the font. A sample of the selected font appears in the Sample box, as shown in Figure 14.2.

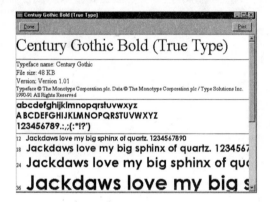

FIGURE 14.2 View a typeface in various sizes to see if it's the font you want to use.

4. Choose the Print button to print the font sample. Choose the Done button to close the sample window.

5. When you finish viewing the fonts, you can add or remove a font (as described next), or you can click the Close button in the title bar to close the window.

Need Hard Disk Space? If you are running low on hard disk space, you can remove some of your fonts using the Fonts window (as described later in this lesson). To see how much space a font takes, choose View, Details. The size of the font files appear in the detailed list.

INSTALLING FONTS FROM DISK

Because all installed fonts are available for use in all Windows applications, you may find that you want to add fonts to your system. When you add a font to Windows NT, it takes up disk space (however, TrueType fonts take up much less space than bitmapped fonts).

To add fonts, you use the Add Fonts dialog box, which offers you the option of connecting to the network as a source for font files. To connect to the network, choose the Network command button. For more information about connecting to a network, see Lesson 16, "Viewing a Network Drive".

To install fonts from a disk, follow these steps:

1. From the desktop, open the Control Panel window by choosing Start, Settings, and Control Panel. Double-click the Fonts folder icon. The Fonts window appears.

2. Choose File, Install New Font. The Add Fonts dialog box appears.

3. In the Drives drop-down list, select the drive from which you want to install the fonts (see Figure 14.3). The fonts on the selected drive appear in the List of Fonts box at the top of the Add Fonts dialog box. Alternatively, choose the Network command button or the folder in which the font is stored from the Folders list.

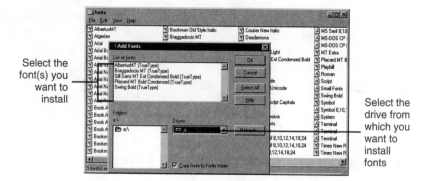

Select the font(s) you want to install

Select the drive from which you want to install fonts

FIGURE 14.3   You can add fonts from a floppy disk, a CD-ROM, or a network drive.

4. In the List of Fonts list box, select the font(s) you want to install. To install multiple fonts, press and hold the Ctrl key and click each of the fonts in the list that you want to install. To install all the fonts in the list box, choose the Select All button.

5. Choose OK, and Windows installs the fonts to the Windows directory (where all the other fonts in your system reside) so they'll be easy to find. Windows returns to the Fonts window, and the newly installed fonts appear highlighted in the Installed Fonts list so you can see them.

6. When you finish, click the Close button in the title bar to close the Fonts window.

DELETING A FONT

Fonts take up space on your hard disk. There may come a time when you want to delete fonts you don't use from memory or from the hard disk. If you decide later that you want to use the deleted fonts, you can always reinstall them using the original program disks. To delete a font, follow these steps:

1. From the desktop, open the Control Panel window by choosing Start, Settings, Control Panel. Double-click the Fonts folder icon. The Fonts window appears.

2. From the list of fonts, select the font(s) you want to remove. You can hold down the Ctrl key and click multiple fonts if you want to delete more than one font at a time.

3. Choose File, Delete. Windows NT displays the Windows Fonts Folder message box.

4. Choose Yes to delete the fonts, or choose No to cancel the command.

5. In the Fonts window, click the Close button in the title bar to exit the window.

 Important!   Do not remove the MS Sans Serif font from the list of Installed Fonts. Windows NT uses this font for the type in most dialog boxes; if you remove the MS Sans Serif, the text in the boxes will be hard to read. You can reinstall the MS Sans Serif font using the Windows NT Workstation installation disks.

In this lesson, you learned how to view, install, and delete fonts. In the next lesson, you'll learn how to print with Windows NT.

15 PRINTING WITH WINDOWS NT

In this lesson, you'll learn to print from an application, control the print job, and connect to a network printer.

PRINTING FROM AN APPLICATION

The steps for printing from any Windows application are very similar. The biggest difference is that some dialog box options change from program to program. Most programs offer a Print icon on the toolbar that you can click to print one copy of the job; although in some programs, the print icon displays the Print dialog box. To print from a Windows application, follow these steps:

1. Choose File, Print, and the Print dialog box appears. Figure 15.1 shows the Print dialog box in the WordPad accessory program.

FIGURE 15.1 Use the Print dialog box to specify printing options.

2. Set any of the printing options described in the following list. (Some applications will offer more specialized options; see a particular application's Help feature if you have questions.)

Print Range   Specify the pages you want to print. For example, you can print all pages, the current page, a range of pages (list the pages in the provided text box), or a selection (which you select before opening the Print dialog box).

Copies   Enter the number of copies to print. Often, you can choose a print order (front to back, for example) and whether to collate the copies or not.

Print to File   Print the document into a file, which you can use to print your document from a computer that doesn't have the program you used to create it. (You then print the file by typing **print** *filename* at the Command Prompt of any computer. All document formatting is preserved.)

Printer   If you have several printers available, you can choose the printer to which you want to send the job.

Properties or **Setup**   Usually leads to a dialog box in which you can set paper size, orientation, paper tray, graphics resolution, and other options specific to your printer.

3. When you're ready to print, choose OK. Windows NT sends the job to the printer.

Printing Errors   If your job doesn't print and you receive an error message from Windows NT, write the message down so you can ask your system administrator about it. Before you do that, though, make sure that the printer is on and there is paper in it.

Print Job   A print job is a document you are printing. Each time you choose OK in the Print dialog box, you are sending a print job to the printer (whether that document contains one page or 40 pages).

WORKING WITH THE PRINT FOLDER

When you print a document, the printer usually begins processing the job immediately. But what if the printer is working on another job that you (or someone else, if you're working on a network printer) sent? When that happens, there is a *print queue* that holds the job until the printer is ready for it.

 Print Queue A holding area for jobs waiting to be printed. If you were to open the contents of the queue, the jobs would appear in the order they were sent to the printer.

You can check on the status of a print job you've sent by looking at the print queue, found in the Printers folder. Figure 15.2 shows a document in the print queue. As you can see, the Print Queue window displays the information about the job. In this figure, the status shows that the printer is offline. If the printer were online, *Printing* would appear in the status column.

FIGURE 15.2 Use the print queue to track your print jobs.

To display the print queue, follow these steps:

1. From the desktop, choose the Start button, and then choose Settings, Printers.

2. In the Printers folder, double-click the printer to which you are printing.

Empty Print Queue? If no jobs appear in the print queue, the job has already been sent to the printer.

CONTROLLING THE PRINT JOB

It's hard to control just one or two jobs because they usually go to the printer too quickly. However, if there are several jobs in the queue, you can control them. For example, you can pause and resume print jobs, and you can delete a job before it prints.

Windows will not let you interfere with other people's print jobs. If you share a network printer, you can control only your own print jobs (unless you have full control access).

Full Control Access The system administrator sets printer permissions that specify the access each user has to that printer. A user with Full Control permission can completely control the print jobs. He or she can modify print settings, printer properties, and users of the printer; pause, resume, and delete a job; and change the order of the print jobs.

PAUSING AND RESUMING THE PRINT QUEUE

You may want to pause the queue and then resume printing later if, for example, the paper in the printer is misaligned or the printer is using the wrong color paper. Pausing the print queue gives you time to correct the problem. To pause the print queue, choose Printer, Pause Printing. To resume printing, choose Printer, Pause Printing a second time to remove the check mark beside the command.

Printer Stalled   If your printer stalls while it's processing your print job, Windows displays the word *stalled* in the printer status line. Choose Printer, Pause Printing to remove the check mark from the command and start printing again. If the printer stalls again, see if there's a problem with the printer (it might be offline or out of paper, for example).

DELETING A PRINT JOB

Sometimes you'll send a document to be printed and then change your mind. For example, you may think of additional text to add to the document or realize you forgot to spell-check your work. In such a case, deleting the print job is easy. Follow these steps:

1. Open the print queue by choosing Start, Settings, and Printers; double-click the printer.

2. Click the job you want to delete.

3. Choose Document, Cancel.

Clear the Queue!   To remove all the files from the print queue, choose Printer, Purge Print Documents. Note, however, that this removes only your own documents from the print queue (unless you have Full Control permission).

INSTALLING A NETWORK PRINTER

You can install a network printer to your workstation so you can easily print without going through the steps of connecting to the network printer. When you install a network printer, you add it to your Printers folder and, therefore, to your printers list in any Print dialog box. When you're ready to print, you choose the network printer from the Print dialog box.

To install a network printer, follow these steps:

1. From the desktop, choose Start, Settings, Printers. The Printers window opens, displaying the printers attached to your computer.

2. Double-click the Add Printer icon in the Printers window. The first screen of the Add Printer Wizard appears as shown in Figure 15.3.

FIGURE 15.3   Add a network printer to your list of printers.

3. Choose the Network Printer Server option and choose the Next button. Follow the directions onscreen to complete installation.

To print from the network printer in any application, choose File, Print. In the Printers area of the Print dialog box, select the printer from the server as the current printer. Choose OK.

In this lesson, you learned how to print from an application, control print jobs, and connect to and install a network printer. In the next lesson, you'll learn how to view a network drive.

16 VIEWING A NETWORK DRIVE

In this lesson, you'll learn to connect to the network, to log on as a different user, and to display shared files on the network.

UNDERSTANDING THE NETWORK

You can use Windows NT Workstation with a number of network server systems, including Novell NetWare, systems that use TCP/IP, Windows NT Server, Microsoft LAN Manager, and IBM LAN Server. Most networks consist of *servers* and *clients*, although some networks consist solely of workstations (called *peer-to-peer* networks). Windows NT Workstation is a client that can attach and share data with various servers and with a peer-to-peer network. When you connect to a network, you gain certain advantages:

- Access to shared resources, such as files and printers

- Access to shared data files

- The capability to send and receive messages with others on the network using a mail program

- The capability to back up your files to the server (see your *system administrator* for more information)

System Administrator   The system or network administrator is the person who oversees your network. The administrator can grant a user permission to access certain
files and resources, troubleshoot problems with the network, and control each computer on the network.

Client/Server   A client/server network is one in which
the NT workstation logs on to and attaches to a server
that controls shared files, printers, and other resources.
Examples of client/server networks include NetWare
and Windows NT Server.

Peer-to-peer   A peer-to-peer network is one in which
all workstations use client operating systems and are
connected and each can share its printer, files, folders,
and other resources. Examples of peer-to-peer networks
include Windows (3.11) for Workgroups, Windows NT
Workstation, and Windows 98.

USING A USERNAME AND PASSWORD

You know that to gain access to Windows NT, you must enter
your username and password, which identify you to the computer, and to the network, if you are attached to one. The
username that appears when you log on to Windows NT and the
password you enter are those that you or the system administrator
created while running Setup. These devices provide security not
only for your work, but for the entire network. Therefore, someone who does not know his or her username and password cannot log on to the network.

After you do log on, you can run applications, print and save files,
share files, and so on. You also have control over who shares the
files and directories on your computer (see Lessons 17, "Sharing
Folders and Files," and 18, "Securing Files and Folders").

Log On To connect to a network, you must log on. When you log on, you're essentially telling the network that you're ready to share its resources. The network uses your logon as a key, of sorts, to identify which resources you may use.

ACCESSING SHARED RESOURCES

Your system administrator grants you and everyone on the network certain rights that control which network files and resources you can access.

CONNECTING TO A NETWORK DRIVE

When you connect to a network drive, you add a whole new set of folders, and files—not to mention other resources—to your working environment. After connecting, you can remain connected to the network while you work, or if you need to access something else, you can disconnect from the network and connect again at any time. (You might disconnect from one server to attach to another server, for example, or disconnect from one network to connect to another.)

To connect to the network, follow these steps:

1. From the desktop, double-click the Network Neighborhood to open that window. Figure 16.1 shows the Network Neighborhood window displaying a peer-to-peer Windows network. Depending on the network you're attached to, your Network Neighborhood window may look different, but the theory and procedure are the same.

This computer

Peer computer
using Windows
3.11 for
Workgroups

FIGURE 16.1   You can access any available network and connect to multiple networks.

2. If you do not see your network in the Network Neighborhood window, double-click the Entire Network icon. The Entire Network window opens, displaying the networks and domains available to you.

3. Double-click the appropriate network (if you're unsure, see your system administrator), and the appropriate domain if applicable, to display the computers, printers, or servers you want to access.

4. To attach to a computer on a peer-to-peer network or to a server, double-click that computer's icon in the Network Neighborhood window. A list of files, folders, printers, and other shared resources appears. Figure 16.2 shows the stepped windows to open to access the folders on a NetWare Server.

   Don't Panic!   If you cannot access a network drive, don't worry. The server might be down for repair, a cable might have become loose, your permission rights might have expired, or some other problem might have occurred. All these are problems that can be easily solved by—you guessed it—your system administrator. Report the problem to him or her.

Double-click Entire Network   Double-click NetWare

Double-click server   Double-click the folder you want to access

FIGURE 16.2   Continue to open windows until you find the folder, file, printer, or other resource you want.

DISPLAYING FILES

You can display files on the network drive in either the Network Neighborhood or the Explorer; either way, you can treat the files and folders just as you would any files on your own hard drive, as long as you've been granted permissions and rights. In the All Folders window, double-click any folder to display its contents. And don't forget that you can use the View menu to display the files by Detail; then you can sort the files by name, type, size, or date. (See Lesson 2, "Working with a Window" for more information on viewing a window's contents.)

In this lesson, you learned to connect to a network drive and to log on as a different user. You also learned how to view files on the network. In the next lesson, you'll learn to share folders and printers, change sharing properties, and view shared files.

Sharing Folders and Files

In this lesson, you'll learn to share folders and printers, change sharing properties, view shared files, and stop sharing resources.

Understanding Group Memberships

Windows NT organizes several groups of users within the workstation and the network, such as Administrators, Power Users, Users, Guests, Backup Operators, and special groups. Each group has certain access rights on the network as defined by the system administrator. For example, the Guests group has very limited access to resources, files, printers, and so on within the network.

The system administrator assigns each person on the network to a group, thus granting that person certain access rights assigned to the group. The following list describes each group and its default network access rights:

- **Administrators** The most powerful group; administrators manage the overall configuration of the workstations and access to most workstation resources.

- **Power Users** Power users have limited access to the users' accounts. A power user can share folders on the network, install and share printers, and create program groups.

- **Users** Members of the Users group can perform everyday tasks with their computers; they can run applications, save and print files, customize their own setup, and so on.

- **Database** Members collect and compile data about the network use and members.

- **Replicator** Members support file replication in a domain.

- **Guests** Guests are often limited to one-time access, which enables them to log on and view limited areas of the network.

- **Backup Operators** The backup operators back up and restore folders and files; therefore, they have the access rights to workstations' files for this purpose.

Of course, the system administrator has the authority to create other groups for specific purposes.

Sharing a Folder

During setup, Windows NT automatically designates one folder (usually named WINNT) as a shared folder. This folder contains your Windows NT files, as well as other pertinent information about your system. The Administrators and Backup Operator groups can access this folder through the network at any time, but they are the only individuals who can access this folder.

You can designate other folders on your computer as *shared* so that others on the network can view and use them. All files within a shared folder are also shared, unless you specifically mark some as not shared. Each shared folder has an outstretched Hand icon next to it in the Windows Explorer's window (see Figure 17.1).

To share a folder, you must be logged on as a member of the Administrators or Power Users group. Follow these steps to mark a folder for sharing:

1. In the Explorer's All Folders window, click on the folder you want to share.

2. Choose File, Properties. That folder's Properties dialog box appears.

Shared drive

Shared folder

FIGURE 17.1   The Hand icon designates a shared folder.

3. Choose the Sharing tab and select the Shared As option (see Figure 17.2).

FIGURE 17.2   Choose to share a folder, and then set limits on who can share it.

4. Fill in the following text boxes:

Share Name   Enter the name a user will specify when he or she wants to connect to the shared folder. (By default, this is the name of the selected folder.)

Comment   (Optional) Enter a note to describe the folder.

Permissions   Permissions deal with specific rights
granted to each group. For more information, see
Lesson 18, "Securing Files and Folders".

5. In the User Limit area, indicate the maximum number of
   users who can connect to the folder at one time; you
   might want to set a limit, for example, to cut down on
   network traffic. Select Maximum Allowed if you don't
   want to set a limit; select Allow and fill in the maximum
   number if you do want to set a limit.

6. Choose OK to share the folder and close the dialog box.
   The outstretched Hand icon now appears next to the
   selected folder in the Explorer folder window.

SHARING A PRINTER

When you share your printer, you're enabling others on the network to connect to your printer and print their own documents.
You designate a shared printer in the Printers folder.

Your Printer   You can only control sharing a printer with
another printer that's directly connected to your computer. You cannot control a printer connected to another
computer or a network printer.

To share a printer, follow these steps:

1. In the Explorer, open the Printers window by double-
   clicking the Printers folder in the left pane. A list of printers appears in the right pane.

2. Select the printer attached to your computer (local
   printer) and choose File, Properties. The printer's Properties dialog box appears.

3. Choose the Sharing tab and select the Shared option button (see Figure 17.3).

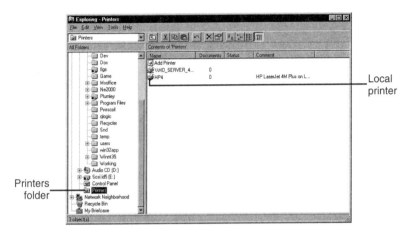

Printers folder

Local printer

FIGURE 17.3   Choose to share in the Properties dialog box.

4. In the Share Name text box, enter a name to represent the printer to other users, if you want, and choose OK.

CHANGING SHARING PROPERTIES

Sharing properties include the number of users allowed to connect to a shared folder and the comment information. You can change these sharing properties at any time, as long as you are logged on to the network as a member of the Administrators or Power Users group. To change sharing properties for folders, follow these steps:

1. In the left pane of the Explorer, select the shared folder for which you want to change properties.

2. Choose File, Properties. The folder's Properties dialog box appears.

3. Choose the Sharing tab and change any of the following sharing properties for the selected folder:

- In the Comment text box, enter a new description or replace the current one.

- In the User Limit area, change the option for the maximum number of users allowed to access the selected folder.

- Choose the New Share button to assign another share name to the folder. In the New Share dialog box, enter a new share name and comment, apply a user limit, and click OK. The dialog box closes, and Windows adds the new share name to the Shared Folder dialog box.

4. Click OK to close the dialog box and put the changes into effect.

SHARING FILES

You can select individual files on your computer and choose whether or not to share the files. You can also determine to what degree you want to share by setting file attributes. Attributes are file markers that indicate information about the file. You can assign the following attributes to a file:

- **Read-Only** Enables others to view the file, but prevents them from changing the file's contents or saving it.

- **Hidden** Hides the file so that it is not listed in the folder. However, you can still access it if you know it's there.

- **Archive** Marks a file for backup.

- **System** Indicates specific files that Windows NT and the computer need to run.

- **Compressed** Marks files that Windows has shrunk. Compressed files take up less space in your computer's memory, but exact a performance penalty.

The system assigns many file attributes in order to protect the file or identify it to the system. However, you can also assign attributes to your files to protect them.

You're Limited When Setting Attributes   If your system uses the Windows NT file system (NTFS), you must have permission to change file attributes. See your system administrator.

To set file attributes, follow these steps:

1. In the Explorer, select the file you want to share.

2. Choose File, Properties. The file's Properties dialog box appears (see Figure 17.4).

Figure 17.4   Set file attributes for individual files.

3. In the Attributes area, select Read-Only to prevent others from changing the file. Select Hidden to keep others from seeing the file.

4. Choose OK to close the dialog box and put the changes into effect.

STOPPING FOLDER SHARING

You can also stop sharing an entire folder, which means it is no longer available on the network. To stop sharing a folder, you must be logged on as a member of the Administrators or Power Users group.

 Data Loss If you choose to stop sharing a folder while other users are connected to it, they may lose their data. NT warns you if any users are connected to the shared folder.

To stop sharing a folder, follow these steps:

1. Select the shared folder.

2. Choose File, Properties and select the Sharing tab.

3. Choose the Not Shared option and choose OK.

In this lesson, you learned to share folders and printers, change sharing properties, and stop sharing your resources. In the next lesson, you'll learn more about granting access and permissions, as well as how to secure files and folders.

Securing Files and Folders

In this lesson, you'll learn to grant permission for file and folder use, edit permission rights, and remove permissions.

Understanding Permissions

You can establish permissions for every file or folder you create and for other shared resources (such as a network printer). Permissions set on files, folders, or other resources limit how much access individual *users* or *groups* of users have to that item. You can limit access so that another user can only view a file or folder, or you can allow unlimited access so that the user can add and delete files and folders, for example. You can even completely deny a person or group access to an object. Most permissions are set for entire groups instead of individual users, because that makes it easier for the system administrator to control overall access.

 Individual versus Group A user is an individual who generally works at one computer on the network (see Lesson 17, "Sharing Folders and Files"). A group is defined within a Windows network as several users who work in a common manner or on similar projects. Often, permissions are granted to the group, which means that each user within the group has the same access to files, folders, and other resources.

Remember these important points when working with permissions:

- You can set permissions only on drives formatted with *Windows NT File System (NTFS)*. Drives formatted with *FAT (File Allocation Table)* don't support Windows security; however, you can set permissions for shared folders on these drives.

- You cannot access or use a folder, file, printer, or ClipBook unless you have permission or belong to a group that has permission.

- Files and subfolders take on the same permissions as their parent folder.

- The creator of a file or folder is the owner; he or she can control access by changing permissions.

- Administrator group members can take ownership of a file or folder and then grant permissions to that file or folder.

 NTFS or FAT?   NTFS is the Windows NT (New Technology) File System used with the Windows NT operating system. FAT (File Allocation Table) is the file system used with MS-DOS, and can also be used with Windows NT.

GRANTING PERMISSION FOR FILE USE

When you set permissions on a file, you're indicating the type of access a group or user has to that file. A file inherits its permissions from the folder if it's created in a folder.

UNDERSTANDING STANDARD FILE PERMISSIONS

You set file permissions from a standard list of permissions. Windows NT uses a set of abbreviations to indicate which permissions are granted. Table 18.1 lists the standard permissions for file access, their abbreviations, and a brief description of each permission.

TABLE 18.1   STANDARD FILE PERMISSIONS

PERMISSION	ABBREVIATION	DESCRIPTION
No Access	(none)	Prevents the user(s) from accessing the file
Read	RX	Permits the user(s) to view the file's data and run the file if it's a program file
Change	RWXD	Permits the user(s) to view the file's data, run it if it's a program file, change data in the file, and delete the file
Full Control	ALL	Permits the user(s) to view the file's data, run it if it's a program file, change data in the file, delete the file, change permissions on the file, and take ownership of the file

 No Access No Access permission overrides all other permissions.

SETTING FILE PERMISSIONS

As mentioned earlier, you can set file permissions only on a drive
formatted with the Windows NT FS (NTFS). In addition, you must
be the owner of the file to set permissions on it, or you must have
been given Full Control permission by the owner. To set permissions, follow these steps:

1. Select the file(s) in the Explorer right pane.

2. Choose File, Properties, and then choose the Security tab.
   Choose the Permissions button and the File Permissions
   dialog box appears (see Figure 18.1).

FIGURE 18.1   The File Permissions dialog box.

3. In the Name list box, select the user or group for whom
   you're setting permissions.

4. Choose the permission from the Type of Access box.
   If you want to remove file permissions instead, click the
   Remove button. If you choose to remove all permissions,
   no one but members of the Administrators group will
   have access to the file or folder.

5. Click OK to close the dialog box.

Special Access To view the permissions set for any user or group, double-click the name in the Name list box. The Special Access dialog box appears, in which you can view and set other permissions.

GRANTING PERMISSION FOR FOLDERS

When you set permission on a folder, you limit the access that groups or users within the network have to that folder and its contents.

UNDERSTANDING FOLDER PERMISSIONS

You can set standard permissions for folders, and Windows NT uses abbreviations to indicate which permissions are used. Table 18.2 lists the standard permissions for folder access, their abbreviations, and a brief description of each.

TABLE 18.2 STANDARD FOLDER PERMISSIONS

PERMISSION	ABBREVIATION	DESCRIPTION
No Access	(none)	Prevents the user(s) from having any access to the folder and its contents
List	RX	Permits the user(s) to view folders, change subfolders, and view subfolders; does not permit access to the folder's files
Read	RX	Permits the user(s) to view filenames and subfolder names, change subfolders, view data in the folder's files, and run programs

PERMISSION	ABBREVIATION	DESCRIPTION
Add	WX	Permits the user(s) to add files and subfolders to the folder; does not permit access to the folder's files
Add and Read	RWX	Permits the user(s) to view filenames and subfolder names, change subfolders, view data in the folder's files, run program files, and add files and subfolders to the folder
Change	RWXD	Permits the user(s) to view filenames and subfolders, change subfolders, view data in the folder's files, run program files, add files and subfolders to the folder, change the folder's files, and delete the folder and its files
Full Control	ALL	Permits the user(s) to view filenames and subfolders, change subfolders, view data in the folder's files, run program files, add files and subfolders to the folder, change the folder's files, delete the folder and its files, change permissions, and take ownership of the folder and its files

CHANGING FOLDER PERMISSIONS

You can change folder permissions only if you're the owner of the folder or if you've been granted permission by the owner. To set or change folder permissions, follow these steps:

1. Select the folder or folders in the Explorer window.

2. Choose File, Properties. The folder's Properties dialog box appears.

3. Choose the Security tab and the Permissions button. The Directory Permissions dialog box appears (see Figure 18.2).

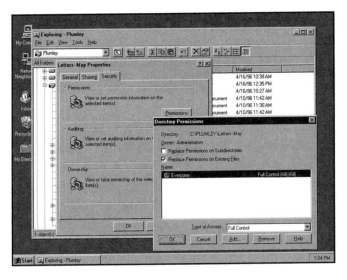

FIGURE 18.2   The Directory Permissions dialog box.

4. Choose one or both of the following check box options:

Replace Permissions on Subdirectories   Applies the permissions you select to all subfolders.

Replace Permissions on Existing Files   Applies the permissions you set to the folder and the files it contains.

5. Select the user or group in the Name list box and choose the permission from the Type of Access drop-down list box.

6. Choose OK to close the dialog box.

In this lesson, you learned how to grant permissions for file and folder use and how to edit and remove those permissions. In the next lesson, you'll learn to send and receive email messages with Microsoft Exchange.

SENDING AND RECEIVING MAIL WITH MICROSOFT EXCHANGE

In this lesson, you'll learn to how to use the address book, send and receive email messages, delete a message, and set options for the mail program in Microsoft Exchange.

UNDERSTANDING MICROSOFT EXCHANGE

You use the Microsoft Exchange program to send and receive mail messages within your network and over the Internet. This can be done through memos, letters, and reports. You can even attach files to a message. All messages sent in Microsoft Exchange travel to a specified directory on your computer—usually USERS\DEFAULT\WPGO, although it may be in another folder, such as \EXCHANGE. Windows NT also refers to the process of sending and receiving mail as Windows Messaging.

When you first start Microsoft Exchange, the Microsoft Exchange Setup Wizard appears to guide you through setting up the program and creating a profile for yourself. Follow the directions and make selections according to the suggestions in the wizard dialog boxes. If you have any questions, ask your mail or network administrator. It is your network administrator who determines whether your organization uses Microsoft Exchange, Outlook Express, or another mail program to handle its users' email.

Internet Service Provider If you're setting up for the Internet, you'll need to know your server's name or IP address and your email address, user account name, and password. You can obtain this information from your Internet service provider (ISP).

You can send and receive messages, delete and print messages, and set options in the Microsoft Exchange program. The following steps walk you through starting and exiting the program.

1. From the desktop, choose the Start button, Programs, and Microsoft Exchange (your Microsoft Exchange may be in a folder, depending on your installation); alternatively, double-click the Inbox icon on your desktop.

2. If you've opened the program before, the Microsoft Exchange window appears (see Figure 19.1). The program opens to the same folder that was open the last time you used Exchange (the folder's name appears in the title bar).

3. To exit the program, choose File, Exit.

Folders list ──

FIGURE 19.1 Use the Microsoft Exchange program to send and receive email.

USING THE ADDRESS BOOK

The Address Book contains the names of the people in your workgroup on the network, as well as people in other domains and other workgroups. Although your system administrator creates and updates the Postoffice Address list, you can add or remove names on the list. You can also use the Address Book to add names to your personal address book.

To open and use the Address Book, follow these steps:

1. In the Microsoft Exchange program, choose Tools, Address Book. The Address Book appears with a list of names in the Postoffice Address List (see Figure 19.2).

 Which Address Book? You can choose either the Postoffice Address List or your own Personal Address Book to view in the Show Names.

FIGURE 19.2 The names of those in your workgroup appear in the Address Book.

2. To view more information about a user on the list (such as his or her phone number, office, or department), double-click the name.

3. To add a name to your personal address book, select the name and click the Add to Personal Address Book button.

4. When you're finished with the Address Book, click the Close button.

SENDING AND READING MESSAGES

You can compose a message, address it, send a carbon copy of it, and specify other options in the Send Note window of the Mail program. In addition, you can read the messages you've sent or received.

To create and send a message, follow these steps:

1. Choose Compose, New Message.

2. In the To text box, enter the name of the person to whom you're sending the message. Alternatively, you can click the To or Cc button and select the recipient's name from the list that appears. Separate multiple names with a semicolon.

3. In the Subject text box, enter the topic of your message.

4. In the message area, type your message. You are not limited to the space you see. As you type, the message scrolls upward in the box so you can fit more text in the message area.

5. Choose File, Send to send the message.

You can format the text in your message by selecting it and choosing the Format menu, and then Font or Paragraph; alternatively, use the formatting toolbar. Display the toolbar by choosing View, Formatting Toolbar.

New mail is displayed in your Inbox in bold type. To read a message you've received, follow these steps:

1. In the Microsoft Exchange program window, click the Inbox to display a list of received messages.

2. Double-click any message to read it.

3. To reply to the message, choose Compose, Reply to Sender. Type your reply and choose File, Send.

Send and Receive To send and receive new mail, click the Tools menu and choose Deliver Now. If you're using more than one mail service, choose the Deliver Now Using command from the Tools menu, and then choose the name of the service you're using from the secondary menu that appears.

Deleting a Message

In order to keep your messages from piling up, you should delete a message when you no longer need it. You can delete a message you've read by choosing File, Delete. In addition, you can delete any message from the message list by dragging it to the Deleted Items folder.

If you change your mind and want the deleted message back, open the Deleted Items folder by double-clicking it. Then select the message you want and drag it to another folder. If any messages remain in the Deleted Items folder when you exit the program, those messages are deleted permanently.

Setting Options

Microsoft Exchange provides several options you can set to customize the program to suit your tastes.

To change program options, follow these steps:

1. In the Microsoft Exchange program, choose Tools, Options. The Options dialog box appears (see Figure 19.3).

2. In the General tab, you can set the following options:

   - When new mail arrives, play a sound, briefly change the pointer, or display a notification message.

   - When deleting items, set the program to warn you before you permanently delete them and/or to empty the deleted items as you exit the program.

- When starting the program, choose a profile for starting the program or choose to enter the profile when you first start the program.

FIGURE 19.3 Change mail options to suit yourself.

3. In the Read tab, specify options for how the program deals with open items and forwarded items.

4. In the Send tab, specify options for sending mail, such as the font used, receipt requests, importance levels of the message, and so on.

5. Use the Services tab to add, remove, copy, and view properties of your mail services, including post office path, Address Book configuration, Internet servers, and IP addresses.

6. In the Delivery tab, specify a location for new mail and the order in which your information services are accessed.

7. Use the Addressing tab to control the post office and personal address lists.

8. Choose OK to close the dialog box.

In this lesson, you learned to use Microsoft Exchange to send and receive mail messages over the network, as well as to delete messages, set mail options, and use the address book. In the next lesson, you'll learn how to use Outlook Express.

USING OUTLOOK EXPRESS

In this lesson you'll learn how to use Outlook Express to send and receive email (electronic mail) and also learn how to use it to participate in newsgroup discussions.

MAIL AND NEWSGROUPS

The two uses for Outlook Express, a part of the Internet Explorer, are email and newsgroups. Email is, like regular mail, private (but not necessarily secure or confidential) correspondence between two or more people (clients). Newsgroups are group discussion areas, somewhat analogous to public bulletin boards, where people can post messages and others respond to those messages.

You need to know some terminology to use either email or newsgroups. Here is a list of needed jargon.

- **Client** You or your computer. In email, the analogy is your home's mailbox is the client while the server is the post office, and the Internet (or other communications medium) is the roads the mail travels on. A client is, more specifically, a program. Outlook Express is a client for the Internet or Internet-like networks. Private email systems, such as America Online (AOL), use proprietary client software.

- **Server** The place that hosts your gateway to newsgroups or acts as a post office for holding your mail until you pick it up. A server can act as both a news and mail server.

- **Newsgroup** A bulletin board-like meeting place in cyberspace where people can exchange ideas and messages. A newsgroup is hosted on a server. That server can be public and accessible by all other servers, or it can be private and require a logon.

- **Email** Private communications between two or more clients.

This lesson is organized into three sections that are related but need not be read at the same time. These sections include

- How to Set up Outlook Express

- Using Outlook Express as an Email Client

- Using Outlook Express as a Newsgroup Client

How to Set up Outlook Express

Launch Outlook Express by double-clicking its desktop icon. If you don't have such an icon, choose Start, Programs, Internet Explorer, Outlook Express. Your screen should resemble Figure 20.1.

Figure 20.1 Outlook Express launched.

Your Outlook Express probably won't have the last two entries in the left pane, but should have the standard entries such as Inbox, Outbox, and so forth. Later in the lesson you'll see how to add newsgroups such as those shown in this figure.

Before using Outlook Express you need to give it specific information about what servers you want it to access and specific client information about your accounts.

THE ADDRESS BOOK

An Address Book is a place to store contact information. Outlook Express can access its Address Book to automatically enter email addresses for you when you create new electronic messages.

To open the Address Book, click its button on the toolbar. To add a new entry, click the New Contact button on the Address Book toolbar. Fill in the any fields you like in the tabbed form that appears.

When you're finished editing your new entry, click OK to save and close the form. Close the Address Book by choosing File, Exit when you're finished adding entries.

EMAIL

To set up an email account, you'll need information somewhat similar to what you need for setting up Dial-Up Networking (see Appendix B, Setting Up the Internet Explorer). If you don't have this information on hand you should be able to get it from the same person who supplied you with your Dial-Up Networking information.

To start the setup process, click Tools, Accounts, and then choose either the News or Mail tab for which type of server you want to set up. This starts the Internet Connection Wizard. Then click Add, Mail to add a new email account (see Figure 20.2). (Mail in this context means email.)

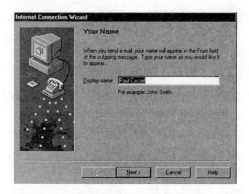

Figure 20.2 This dialog box is the start of setting up a new email account.

The third step in the wizard, shown in Figure 20.3 is the critical step where you need to specify your server addresses. These addresses can be named with letters, as you see in Figure 20.3, or numerically in an IP address such as 193.283.282.1.

Figure 20.3 One of the critical dialog boxes for setting up a new account is this one, where you tell Outlook Express what your server addresses are.

The next dialog box is equally important. You need to tell Outlook Express your logon name and password for this server. The password appears as asterisks for a security measure. If you get a security error when you try to logon to your email account, return to this dialog box by choosing Tools, Accounts, Mail, from the main Outlook Express menu, and then highlight the account, choose Properties, and double-check the entries in this and the previous dialog boxes.

Finish entering your personal information in the dialog boxes, and then exit the Setup Wizard for email. To exit the Accounts dialog box, click Close.

The Setup Wizard allows you to have as many email accounts as you want to use with Outlook Express, but most people have only one.

NEWSGROUPS

Setting up a newsgroup account is similar to setting up an email account, but the details vary. Again, you'll need technical information from your system administrator or Internet service provider (ISP).

Launch Outlook Express and choose Tools, Accounts. This time choose Add, News. Again enter your display name and email name. The third dialog box asks you what your news server is; this is the information you'll need to get from your ISP or system administrator. A news server address is visible in Figure 20.4.

Figure 20.4 You'll need to get your server's address from your system administrator or ISP.

If you want to create an account for a private news server, you'll most likely have to log on. Get your logon name and password from the administrator of that server, check the My News Server Requires Me to Log On check box (see Figure 20.4), and then click Next. You'll see a logon name and password screen similar to the one for your email.

If you'll be using a public server only, such as the Usenet of the Internet, you won't need either a logon name or a password. In either case, click Next until you complete the wizard, and then click Close to exit the Accounts dialog box. You're all set up. Refer to Figure 20.1 to see an installation of Outlook Express with two news servers, Microsoft News and Usenet. After you set up a news account, you'll see an entry in the left pane of the Outlook Express dialog box.

USING OUTLOOK EXPRESS AS AN EMAIL CLIENT

Using Outlook Express is much easier than setting it up. To use Outlook Express to pick up your mail, be sure that you're connected to the Internet using either your local network or a dial-up account (see Appendix B, "Setting Up the Internet Explorer"). After launching the program, Outlook Express picks up your mail and deposits it into your Inbox. An Inbox is a folder and your email messages are files in that folder.

Figure 20.5 shows Outlook Express with several emails in the Inbox. Note the Inbox is highlighted in the left pane and the emails themselves are in the upper-right pane. Double-click on any email message to open it in its own window. To read your email in the bottom-right pane , highlight it, and Outlook Express will display it, as you can see in Figure 20.5.

To reply to an email, highlight it and click the Reply button on the toolbar.

Figure 20.5 You can display an email in its own window by double-clicking it or you can display it in Outlook Express by highlighting it.

To compose a new email, click the Compose button on the toolbar. Outlook Express will bring up an email form with places for an addressee, a subject, and copies. After you're finished creating your email, click the Send button on the toolbar. If you want to send the mail later on, choose File, Send Later. Outlook Express will place the email in the Outbox and by default send it next time you launch the program. You can force the sending items from the Outbox by clicking the Send and Receive button on the toolbar when you have any email folder highlighted.

You can drag Inbox emails to folders on the left pane. You also can create new folders in the Inbox using the File, Folder, New Folder commands. And, you can delete emails by highlighting them and pressing the Del key.

REMOVING OR MOVING EMAIL MESSAGES

To remove email messages, highlight them then press Del, or click the Delete button on the toolbar. This moves messages to the Deleted folder. You can also drag messages to existing folders or make new folders using names of your choice by choosing File, Folder, New Folder.

If you want to remove messages permanently, open the Deleted folder, highlight the messages you want to purge, and then press Del or click the Delete button on the toolbar.

You can also export messages outside of Outlook Express by opening them, and then choosing File, Save As from the menu. You can export all or some of your messages in batch by choosing File, Export with any mail folder highlighted. File, Export also allows you to export your Address Book.

Using Outlook Express as a Newsgroup Client

While connected to the Internet or a private network, if that's where your server exists, click on any news account you've created. If this is the first time you've used this account, Outlook Express will download a list of newsgroups existing on this server. This occurs automatically, but Outlook Express will ask for your approval before proceeding. Because you can't use a news server without downloading its newsgroups, agree to the process. This will take from a few seconds to a few minutes.

After the download completes, you'll have a list of newsgroups for the server. To participate in a newsgroup, double-click on it in the list box. This will give you a subscription to the newsgroup. Figure 20.6 shows the list box of newsgroups for Usenet with some already subscribed newsgroups visible under the Usenet heading in the left pane. A subscribed newsgroup appears as a selection under that news server in the left pane of Outlook Express. This makes returning to such newsgroups much faster.

Note there are three tabs and a text box to narrow down the list of groups. For example, if you only want to see groups containing the word Mercedes, enter that word in the text box above the list of newsgroups.

Figure 20.6 The newsgroup list box has a server selection panel, three tabs, a list of groups, and a text box to narrow the number of groups displayed.

To visit a group that you have subscribed to, make sure that you're logged on to the network (such as the Internet), and then click on the group. Outlook Express will download the headers for this newsgroup. Headers are functionally similar to the subject lines of emails. Figure 20.7 shows some downloaded headers.

Figure 20.7 Headers are similar to the subject lines of emails and serve the same purpose.

To read any message, double-click it to place it in its own window or just click it once to display it in the lower pane of the right panel. Messages are stacked in related threads that you can expand (refer to Figure 20.7).

To reply to a message, highlight it, and then click on the Reply to Group button to reply publicly (post to a newsgroup) or Reply to Author to send a private reply by email. Figure 20.8 shows a Reply to Group being composed.

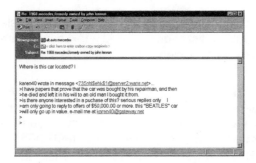

Figure 20.8 By default, your replies include a quote of the replied to message so your correspondents can keep track of your conversations.

To create a new newsgroup message, highlight the newsgroup you want to post to, click the Compose Message button on the toolbar, fill out the message, and then click the Post button to post it immediately. To delay posting, choose File, Send Later. This places your message in the Outbox. You can force the sending items from the Outbox by clicking the Send and Receive button on the toolbar when you have any email folder highlighted.

THE TWIT FILTER

Outlook Express has a feature allowing you to treat news and email messages differently depending on the rules you establish. Because people use these rules primarily to filter out unwanted messages, this capability is generally known on the Internet as a twit filter, although Microsoft doesn't specifically refer to these filters by that common name.

To see the dialog boxes for setting message rules, choose Tools, Inbox Assistant for email, or choose Tools, Newsgroup Filters for newsgroups. Both venues work similarly. You can add what types of messages Outlook Express should watch out for and what to do when they're found.

Figure 20.9 shows an Inbox Assistant set up to remove sexually-oriented mass mailings that some users might find in their email inboxes.

Figure 20.9 Here the Inbox Assistant is set up to watch for, and then remove email messages with certain keywords indicating salacious content in the subject line or from any mail sent from a server with the word *hotmail* in it.

To add a new rule, click the Add button (refer to Figure 20.9). This brings up the Properties dialog box shown in Figure 20.10. Add the rules you want, and then instruct Outlook Express what it should do when such messages appear. Click OK and you've set up your own filters.

CLEANING UP OLD MESSAGES

After a surprisingly short period, your newsgroups can grow huge in downloaded messages or even just message headers. To clean up old messages, highlight any newsgroup or server, and then choose File, Clean Up Files, from the main menu.

Figure 20.10 This rule will watch for mail from a certain person, and then delete it from the server without downloading it into the Inbox.

You'll be presented with a dialog box allowing you to delete message bodies or entire messages, or just compact your folders. This lesson shows you how to set up Outlook Express for new email and newsgroup accounts(and explains how to use those accounts for email and newsgroup participation. In the next lesson you'll learn how to use the Internet Explorer and the Active Desktop.

Using the Internet Explorer and the Active Desktop

In this lesson you'll learn to use the Internet Explorer and Active Desktop.

Surfing the World Wide Web

This chapter uses Internet Explorer version 4 for its example, although Internet Explorer version 5 is similar in features. After you've learned the fundamentals of 4, you also have mastered them for 5. A *browser* is a program for displaying multimedia content on one of the Internet's subsystems called the *World Wide Web* (WWW). Today such content can exist not only on the Internet, but on your company's private network or even your own personal computer; however, most people use browsers, such as Internet Explorer (IE) on the Internet.

You can use a browser to access and display files on your local network or the Internet. A *network* is a connected group of computers created to share files or resources. Many businesses use networks, although some home users with more than one computer find them convenient too. But, for most part, home users connect through a modem even if they are connected to a network.

There are two basic ways people get to the Internet. They either go through their local network using a gateway or dial up using a modem. If you use a gateway, Internet access will be transparent, but you might need your system administrator to give you the necessary permissions.

If you need to dial up using a modem, you'll need to use Dial-Up Networking to establish your connection. Before using Dial-Up Networking, you'll have to set up your account. For details on this, see Appendix B, "Setting Up the Internet Explorer."

After you've established your account, it's time to get online. Here are the steps. (Remember, if you're accessing the Internet through your local network, skip to step 4).

1. Open My Computer. Double-click on Dial-Up Networking. If necessary choose a dial-up account using the top combo box.

2. Click the Dial button.

3. Enter your logon name and password if prompted. You might just log on automatically depending on your Dial-Up Networking settings.

4. Locate the Internet Explorer icon on your desktop and double-click it.

By default, Internet Explorer, will start for the first time at a registration page—this registration is optional. Thereafter it will automatically go to a page Microsoft has established for this purpose, unless you change its setting. Figure 21.1 shows the launched browser at Microsoft's IE4 page. You can see the address or URL (the page's address) for this page in the Address combo box just below the title bar.

 URL, uniform resource locator A standardized form of addressing Web pages, which is valid for computers, networks, and the Internet itself.

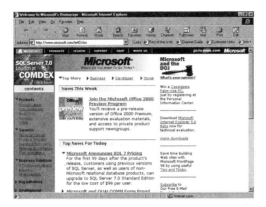

Figure 21.1 Microsoft has a home page set up for IE4 users.

Using Internet Explorer

There is an enormous variety of sites that you can visit on the Web); each site has a URL. But, the problem most people face with the Web isn't a lack of interesting sites, but the ability to find those sites and keep them organized so they can revisit them easily.

Internet Explorer supplies several tools to make these location and organization chores easier.

- A searching facility to locate sites by keyword.

- A history facility allowing you to return to recently visited sites.

- A storage place that permits you to save favorite site addresses for later.

- A fast access facility that allows you to immediately go to a site if you know the address.

Setting Your Own Home Page

Microsoft has programmed Internet Explorer to launch with the Microsoft's Web site loaded. You can set Internet Explorer to show any page you know the address of, or even a blank page. To do this, choose Tools, Internet Options, from the main menu. Make sure the General tab is at the very top. Either click one of the three buttons shown to set that home page option, or enter a URL directly in the text box above the three buttons.

SEARCHING THE WEB

Click the Search button on Internet Explorer's toolbar. If this is your first search, you might need to tell Internet Explorer which search engine to use. Pull down the Choose a Search Engine combo box to tell Internet Explorer which specific search engine to use. You can choose any of them for starters. If you don't like your results, you can always change engines later on.

You'll now see a place to enter your search criteria. Enter your criteria, for example **Porsche cars** as in the example shown in Figure 21.2. Press Enter after entering your criteria and the search engine will return one or more Web sites matching your search criterion.

Keep in mind that you can vary which search engine you use, so when searching, your screen might not be identical to the one shown in Figure 21.2.

Figure 21.2 The Search button will open a panel with a place to enter search criteria.

When you've found a site you want to visit in the Search panel, click on its name (which is underlined to represent that it is a link or shortcut to a Web page). It will appear in the regular panel. When you want to close the search panel, click on the Search button again.

RETURNING TO RECENTLY VISITED SITES

Click the History button on the toolbar to open a panel showing a hierarchical listing of recently visited sites. This panel works similarly to the left panel of the Windows Explorer in that it's expandable and collapsible (see Lesson 10, "Viewing Drives, Folders, and Files with the Windows Explorer"). Note the Microsoft site first in the history list is expanded in Figure 21.3 with the actual pages previously visited under the main Microsoft site listing. As with Search, click on any of the sites to return to them. You can resize any panel in Internet Explorer by dragging the borders, which is similar to resizing panels in Windows Explorer.

Figure 21.3 The history list is similar in structure to the left panel of Windows Explorer. You can expand or collapse entries like folders and files.

Close the History panel by clicking on the History toolbar button again.

SAVING FAVORITE PLACES

The history entries expire in about three weeks by default. If you want to keep a site in permanent storage (until you choose to delete it), Internet Explorer offers an easy way.

After finding a site you want to return to, click the Favorites menu, and then click Add To Favorites. That brings up a dialog box allowing you to edit the site title and either store it in an existing folder or make a new folder. Figure 21.4 shows this dialog box fully expanded to show current folders.

Figure 21.4 Favorites are sites that remain in storage until you choose to remove them.

FAST DIRECT ACCESS TO SITES

If you know the URL of a site, you can tell Internet Explorer to go there directly. For example, to visit the site www.mrshowbiz.com, press Ctrl+O (the letter O, not the number zero) and enter the address. Figure 21.5 shows this dialog box.

Using the Address Bar You can also visit a Web site by clicking in the address bar of Internet Explorer, and then entering a URL . The address bar is the space on the toolbar where the current URL displays.

Figure 21.5 Ctrl+O is the express train to any Web site.

Click OK or press Enter after entering the address and Internet Explorer will take you there directly.

USING THE ACTIVE DESKTOP

Activating the Active Desktop feature allows your computer to act very similarly, whether you're online surfing the Web or moving through your local computer or network.

To start the Active Desktop, right-click the desktop anywhere off an icon. This brings up a context menu with three entries, as shown in Figure 21.6.

Figure 21.6 The selected entry in this context menu will toggle the Active Desktop on and off.

Choose View As Web Page to activate the desktop. Choose Customize My Desktop to launch a dialog box with several options, as shown in Figure 21.7.

Figure 21.7 This dialog box is also available by clicking the Web tab in the Display Properties dialog box.

Note the Folder Options button. This allows you to highly customize all the settings for your Active Desktop. Using the settings in the dialog box that comes up if you click this button, you can make your desktop behave like a Web site. For example, the Web Style option button on the General tab converts your desktop icons to launch with a single-click just like Web links. Figure 21.8 shows the View tab of the Folder Options dialog box. Figure 21.9 shows the results of applying some of the more important settings within that tab.

In this lesson you learned how to navigate the Web using the Internet Explorer, search the Web, return to your recently visited sites, save sites permanently, move directly to a site, and configure your desktop to use the Active Desktop feature. In the next lesson you'll learn how to use the Event Viewer—Windows NT's troubleshooter.

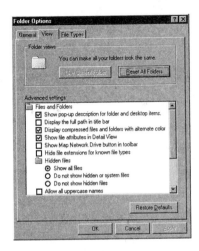

Figure 21.8 This dialog box is the heart of customizing your Active Desktop.

Hand-
shaped ──
cursor

Figure 21.9 Each of the icons on the desktop now will launch with a single-click. Note that they are underlined to indicate they act as links. The mouse cursor over the Internet Explorer link appears as a hand, indicating a single-click will launch the program.

22

LESSON

USING THE
EVENT VIEWER

In this lesson, you'll learn to use the Event Viewer to troubleshoot problems you might have with Windows NT, the network, or your system.

UNDERSTANDING THE EVENT VIEWER

The Event Viewer is a program that monitors your system and records failures and problems in event logs. If, for example, a driver failed to load during startup or an application had a file error, the Event Viewer would record this event so you could study the problem.

Table 22.1 lists the common terms you'll see in the Event Viewer window.

TABLE 22.1   EVENT VIEWER TERMS

TERM	DESCRIPTION
Category	A classification that describes the event (such as Logon, Policy Change, or Account Management)
Computer	The computer name where the event occurred
Event	An identification number assigned to each event
Source	The software or system component that logged the event
User	The name of the user logged on at the time of the event

To start and quit the Event Viewer, follow these steps:

1. From the desktop, choose the Start button and then choose Programs, Administrative Tools, and Event Viewer. The Event Viewer System Log appears (see Figure 22.1).

FIGURE 22.1   The Event Viewer starts recording events from the first time you turn on your Windows NT Workstation.

2. To exit the Event Viewer, choose Log, Exit.

VIEWING EVENT LOGS

You can view three different logs in the Event Viewer: System, Security, and Application. The System Log records events such as hardware, driver, and other system component problems. The Security Log records events such as breaches to security (attempts to log on to the system, for example). The Application Log records all application events, such as file errors, lockups, and so on.

To view an event log, follow these steps:

1. Open the Log menu.

2. Choose System, Security, or Application. A check mark appears beside the selected log, and the log name in the Event Viewer title bar changes.

3. You can choose View, Oldest First or View, Newest First to look at the logs in a different order by date. By default, the view shows the most recent events first.

4. To update the events shown in any Event Viewer log, choose View, Refresh.

The Event Viewer displays an icon to the left of each event to classify it. Table 22.2 describes the icons that appear in the Event Viewer log.

TABLE 22.2   EVENT VIEWER ICONS

ICON DESCRIPTION	EVENT TYPE	REPRESENTS
Stop sign	Error	A problem that leads to loss of data or functions
Exclamation point	Warning	Something that may cause future problems
Lowercase i	Information	An event that describes successful operation of major services
Padlock	Success Audit	Successfully audited security access attempt
Key	Failure Audit	Unsuccessfully audited security access attempt

 Audit   The audit is a tracking service that follows the activities of users at the workstation and records selected events in the security log.

VIEWING EVENTS

You can filter the events in a log so that the Event Viewer displays only specific characteristics. In addition, you can search for specific events, and you can view descriptions and details of the events in any log.

FILTERING THE EVENTS

Filtering events is a way of displaying only the specific events you want to view. To filter events, follow these steps:

1. In the Event Viewer, pull down the Log menu and select the log you want to view.

2. Choose View, Filter Events. The Filter dialog box shown in Figure 22.2 appears.

FIGURE 22.2   Choose specific characteristics to narrow the number and type of events displayed.

3. In the View From area, choose First Event to view events beginning with the first event ever logged on your system. Or, choose Events On to display only the events on and after the date or time you indicate in the text boxes.

4. In the View Through area, choose Last Event to view events through the most recent event on the system. Or, choose Events On to display events that were logged from the date and time you specified in the View From area to the date and time you specify in the View Through area.

5. In Types, deselect any type of event you do not want to view. By default, all event types are selected.

6. In the Source drop-down list, select the type of software (usually a device driver) you want to use to view the event.

7. In the Category drop-down list, choose one category to view only.

View User/Computer?   In the User and Computer text boxes, you can choose to view events logged to a specific user or on a specific computer if you're not viewing your own, and if you're logged in as a member of the Administrators group.

8. Click OK to apply the filtering options to the log. Figure 22.3 shows a system log with the information events filtered out.

Date	Time	Source	Category	Event	User	Computer
3/4/96	11:23:33 AM	Print	None	20	SYSTEM	DIRECTOR
3/4/96	11:19:58 AM	Service Control Mgr	None	7026	N/A	DIRECTOR
3/4/96	10:41:52 AM	Service Control Mgr	None	7026	N/A	DIRECTOR
3/4/96	10:41:50 AM	Server	None	2504	N/A	DIRECTOR
3/4/96	10:41:35 AM	Service Control Mgr	None	7000	N/A	DIRECTOR
3/4/96	10:37:33 AM	Service Control Mgr	None	7026	N/A	DIRECTOR
3/4/96	10:37:30 AM	Server	None	2504	N/A	DIRECTOR
3/4/96	10:37:14 AM	Service Control Mgr	None	7000	N/A	DIRECTOR
3/4/96	10:30:35 AM	Service Control Mgr	None	7026	N/A	DIRECTOR
3/4/96	10:30:32 AM	Server	None	2504	N/A	DIRECTOR
3/4/96	10:30:19 AM	Service Control Mgr	None	7000	N/A	DIRECTOR
3/4/96	10:25:01 AM	Service Control Mgr	None	7023	N/A	DIRECTOR
3/4/96	10:25:01 AM	Service Control Mgr	None	7026	N/A	DIRECTOR
3/4/96	10:25:01 AM	Server	None	2503	N/A	DIRECTOR
3/4/96	10:25:00 AM	Service Control Mgr	None	7001	N/A	DIRECTOR
3/4/96	10:24:59 AM	Service Control Mgr	None	7001	N/A	DIRECTOR
3/4/96	10:24:59 AM	Service Control Mgr	None	7002	N/A	DIRECTOR
3/4/96	10:24:52 AM	Service Control Mgr	None	7001	N/A	DIRECTOR
3/4/96	10:24:52 AM	Service Control Mgr	None	7000	N/A	DIRECTOR
3/4/96	10:24:52 AM	Nwlnkipx	None	9503	N/A	DIRECTOR

Event Viewer - System Log on \\DIRECTOR (Filtered)
Log View Options Help

FIGURE 22.3   Filter out some events to make it easier to view problems.

Finding Events

Another way to view specific events is to use the Find feature, which is especially useful if your log is extremely large. You can, for example, search for all error events in all sources. To search for a specific event in a log, follow these steps:

1. In the Event Viewer, select the log you want to view.

2. Choose View, Find. The Find dialog box appears (see Figure 22.4).

Figure 22.4   Use the Find dialog box to find specific event types.

3. In the Types area, click the necessary check boxes so that only the events you're looking for have a check mark in the check box.

4. (Optional) To search through only a specific source or category, select the one you want from the Source or the Category drop-down list.

5. Choose Find Next when you're ready to search. The dialog box closes and highlights the next instance of the event type you're searching for.

6. Press F3 to find the next instance of the event type you described in the Find dialog box. Continue pressing F3 to search for the next instance.

Viewing Details of an Event

When you find some events (particularly a warning or an error, for example), you'll want to view more details of the event to get a clearer picture of what's going on with your system. You can view a text description of a selected event. However, be aware that some events generate more detail than others.

To view the details of an event, follow these steps:

1. In the Event Viewer, select the event you want to view.

2. Choose View, Detail. The Event Detail dialog box appears (see Figure 22.5).

 Shortcut Double-click an event to quickly open the Event Detail dialog box.

Figure 22.5 You can view a description and other information about the event.

 0000? The information in the Data area of the Event Detail dialog box is hex data generated by the source of the event record. Usually, only a support technician familiar with the source can interpret this data. However, you can read the text description of the event and perhaps get a clue to your system's problem.

CHANGING EVENT LOG SETTINGS

You can change the settings of any Event Log. You can set the maximum log size, you can overwrite events as needed, and you can change other options as described in the following list:

- **Maximum Log Size**   Specify the maximum log file size, in kilobytes.

- **Overwrite Events as Needed**   Select this option to ensure that there will be space for new events when the log is full.

- **Overwrite Events Older than *X* Days Old**   Select this option to keep a log for a specific number of days (from 1–365).

- **Do Not Overwrite Events**   Select this to retain all events when log is full.

- **Default**   Click Default to restore default settings in the dialog box.

To change Event Log settings, follow these steps:

1. In the Event Viewer, choose Log, Log Settings. The Event Log Settings dialog box appears.

2. In Change Settings, select the log you want to change.

3. Change the settings as described in the previous list.

4. Click OK to close the dialog box.

In this lesson, you learned to use the Event Viewer to troubleshoot problems you might have with Windows NT, the network, or your system. In the next lesson, you'll learn how to configure and use NT's multimedia features.

23 WORKING WITH MULTIMEDIA

In this lesson, you'll learn to use CD Player, Media Player, and the Sound Recorder to work with multimedia.

USING THE CD PLAYER

Windows NT provides a CD Player program that works with your CD-ROM drive so that you can play audio CDs while you're working. Like a regular advanced CD player, Windows' CD Player contains features such as random play, programmable playback order, and the capability to save play lists. If you save a play list, you don't have to re-create it each time you insert a CD, which means you can skip over songs you don't want to play or you can play the songs in a specific order. To use the CD Player, follow these steps:

1. From the desktop, choose the Start button, Programs, Accessories, Multimedia, and then CD Player. The CD Player window appears (see Figure 23.1).

FIGURE 23.1 Use the CD Player to play audio CDs on your computer.

2. Insert the CD into the drive, and the CD Player scans the CD. If you have played this CD before, the program fills in the artist, title, and track in the appropriate text boxes. If Autoplay is turned on, the CD will begin to play automatically after you insert it.

3. Click the Play button to play the CD, if Autoplay did not start it for you. To pause the CD, click the Pause button. To resume playing the CD, click the Play button again.

Skip Tracks   Choose the Track drop-down list to display a list of tracks on the CD. Select a track and the CD Player skips to that track.

4. If this is the first time you've played this CD, you can set up the play list by choosing Disc, Edit Play List. The CD Player: Disc Settings dialog box appears. Enter the artist's name and the CD title. In Play List, you can specify the order in which you want to play the tracks. Choose OK when you finish entering the settings.

5. To control the volume (you must have a sound card), choose View, Volume Control. The Volume Control box appears. Slide the bar up to increase the volume or down to decrease it.

Volume Control   The Volume Control box in the Accessories window works the same as the Volume Control in the CD Player. When the CD Player is on, you cannot use the Volume Control box in the Multimedia folder.

6. To change the play order of the tracks, open the Options menu and choose Random Order. The CD Player mixes up the order of the tracks for you.

> **Change Tracks**   Click the Previous Track button to play the previous track on the play list. Click the Next Track button to play the next track on the play list. Click the Skip Backward button to move backward within a track. Click the Skip Forward button to move forward within a track.

7. Click the Stop button to stop playing your CD.

8. Click the Eject button to eject your CD.

USING THE MEDIA PLAYER

The Media Player program enables you to play such multimedia files as Windows-compatible multimedia voice, animated video files, and MIDI-based music files. You might use the Media Player, for example, to view books, cartoons, or encyclopedia clips on CD-ROM. Figure 23.2 shows the Media Player. Depending on your computer, your Media Player may or may not look and work like the one described here.

> **MIDI File**   A MIDI (Musical Instrument Digital Interface) file contains electronic instructions for playing music using different instrumental voices.

To use the Media Player, follow these steps:

1. From the desktop, choose the Start button. Select Programs, Accessories, Multimedia, and then select the Media Player. The Media Player opens.

2. Open the Device menu and indicate which of the following you're going to play:

    CD Audio   Choose an audio CD to play.

    Video for Windows   Choose a video sequence (AVI); NT supports 8-bit, 16-bit, and 24-bit color image files.

If you choose a Video device, the Open dialog box appears. (If you choose CD Audio, you can insert an audio CD, and the Media Player begins playing the music.)

FIGURE 23.2 Use the Media Player to play sounds, video sequences, and even CDs.

3. In the Open dialog box, choose the drive, folder, and filename of the file you want to use. Then click OK.

4. In the Media Player, click the Play button to play the file.

5. To change the volume, choose Device, Volume Control. The Volume box appears. Adjust the volume by sliding the bar up for more volume or down for less volume.

Rewind and Fast Forward Drag the slider to the left to rewind to the previous selection mark or to the beginning of the file. Drag the slider to the right to fast forward to the next selection mark or to the end of the file.

6. Click the Stop button to stop playing your file.

7. Click the Eject button to eject your file (if it's on CD).

To play a specific selection, move the slider to the location where you want to start playing the selection. Click the Start Selection button to mark the beginning of the selection. Likewise, you can move the slider to the location where you want to stop playing the selection and click the End Selection button to mark the end of the selection. Press Alt+P or click the Play button to perform the selection you specified.

USING THE SOUND RECORDER

The Sound Recorder program lets you record, modify, and mix sounds. Figure 23.3 shows the Sound Recorder.

FIGURE 23.3   Use the Sound Recorder to create and modify sound files.

To be able to record sounds, you must have some type of input device such as a microphone or a MIDI instrument. You must also have a sound card, even if you're just recording a CD to a file.

To record a sound, follow these steps:

1. From the desktop, choose the Start button. Select Programs, Accessories, Multimedia, and then select the Sound Recorder. The Sound Recorder opens.

2. Choose File, New from the Sound Recorder menu bar. The Sound Selection dialog box appears.

3. Choose the Save As button and enter a name in the text box. Specify the file format and attributes. Choose OK.

4. In the Sound Recorder, click the Record button to begin recording.

5. Speak, play music, or make whatever sound you want to record into the microphone.

6. When you finish recording, click the Stop button to stop recording.

7. Choose File, Save As from the Sound Recorder menu bar to save the sound file. Enter a name and location for the sound file and choose OK.

To play a sound using the Sound Recorder, follow these steps:

1. From the desktop, choose Start, Programs, Accessories, Multimedia, and Sound Recorder.

2. Choose File, Open, and the Open dialog box appears.

3. Choose the drive, folder, and filename of the sound file you want to play. Then click the Open button.

4. Click the Play button in the Sound Recorder window to play the sound. As the sound plays, you see a visual representation of the sound waves in the Wave box, and the slide bar moves from the left to the right.

In this lesson, you learned to use the CD Player, Media Player, and the Sound Recorder. In the next lesson, you'll learn to use the Command Prompt.

24 USING THE COMMAND PROMPT

In this lesson, you'll learn how to use the Command Prompt, get help in a Command Prompt window, use DOS commands, and exit the Command Prompt.

UNDERSTANDING THE COMMAND PROMPT

The Command Prompt is a character-based interface to Windows NT. What that means is that you can type in commands at a prompt to perform tasks, to run applications, and to otherwise control the computer, your files and directories, and your programs.

You can use the Command Prompt to perform the following operations:

- Start applications usually associated with other operating systems (such as Windows NT, Windows 3.11, MS-DOS, or POSIX-compliant operating systems)

- Issue commands, including most MS-DOS-like commands and some new NT commands, as well as many network commands for using resources and administration

- Use the edit commands on the Control menu for cutting and pasting data between applications

Command Prompt   The Command Prompt in Windows NT does not use MS-DOS; it actually uses a similar interface called the Windows NT Command Prompt. If you type **ver** (for version) at the Command Prompt, NT responds with the prompt (Windows NT Workstation 4.0.) The prompt looks and acts like the Command Prompt you see in other operating systems, such as MS-DOS.

To start and quit the Command Prompt, follow these steps:

1. From the desktop, choose the Start button. Select Programs and from the Programs menu, choose Command Prompt. The Command Prompt window appears. As you can see in Figure 24.1, the default Command Prompt is the current drive and directory.

Control menu button

Command Prompt

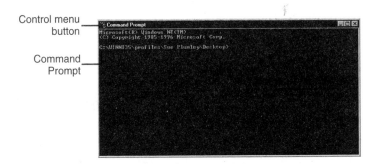

FIGURE 24.1   The Command Prompt window.

2. When you're ready to quit the Command Prompt, exit all applications (using each application's quit or exit command). Then type exit at the prompt and press Enter. You return to the Windows NT Desktop.

USING COMMANDS

There are hundreds of commands you can use at the Command Prompt and if you have questions about any of the commands, you can use the Help feature as described in the next section. If you already know the DOS operating system, you can use many of the DOS commands you're used to. In addition, many NetWare commands work in the NT Command Prompt window.

Before I go into telling you about specific commands, though, let me tell you about a few things that relate to all commands. *Syntax* is the order in which you must type the command and any additional elements (command name, parameters, switches, and values) that follow it. A *parameter* is information that defines the object on which you're performing a command, and a *switch* modifies how the command is performed. In the command `dir` `*.doc` `/s`, for example, `dir` is the command, `*.doc` is the parameter, and `/s` is the switch. This command tells Windows NT to list a directory of all documents with a DOC extension found in all subdirectories.

Table 24.1 describes a few of the more common commands you may find a use for.

TABLE 24.1   COMMON COMMANDS

COMMAND	PARAMETER(S)	FUNCTION
break		Stops the previous command
cd\		Changes to the root directory
cd	*subdirectory*	Changes to the specified subdirectory
cls		Clears the screen
copy	*file drive/directory*	Copies the specified file to the specified drive or directory

continues

TABLE 24.1   CONTINUED

COMMAND	PARAMETER(S)	FUNCTION
dir		Displays a list of files and subdirectories in the current directory
del	*file(s)*	Deletes one or more specified file(s)
move	*file drive/directory*	Moves the specified file to the specified drive or directory
ren	*oldfilename newfilename*	Renames the file specified by *oldfilename* with the name specified by *newfilename*
start		Starts a separate window in which to run a command or program
edit		Starts the MS-DOS Editor, in which you can create and edit text files
exit		Closes the Command Prompt window

To use a command, first start a new command session by clicking the MS-DOS icon in the Program Manager's Main program group window (as covered in the previous section). Type the command and any additional parameters or switches at the Command Prompt, and then press Enter. Figure 24.2 shows the Command Prompt window with the results of the command dir *., which displays a list of directories only.

FIGURE 24.2 The DIR command offers many parameters and switches that enable you to display the directories on your computer.

Slow Down! When you list a directory, it usually scrolls by so quickly that you can't read everything on the list. To fix that, type **dir /p**. The /p stands for pause, which tells Windows NT to pause the listing a screen at a time so you can see everything in the list. When the list is paused, you can press any key to continue to the next screen.

Error Message If, after entering a command, you receive a message that says the name specified is not recognized, you may have misspelled the command or used the wrong parameters. Try entering the command again. If you continue to have problems, check the online Help system, which you'll learn about next.

GETTING HELP

Just as you can get online help by using the commands in Windows NT's Help menu, you can get online help for all commands at the Command Prompt. Table 24.2 describes the common Help commands you can type at the Command Prompt.

TABLE 24.2   HELP COMMANDS

COMMAND	FORM OF HELP PROVIDED
help	Displays names of the 32-bit operating system commands
command /?	Gives you help on the syntax, parameters, and switches for the command you enter (for example, if you type **dir /?**, it gives you help on the dir command)
net help	Lists the names of the network commands
net help	Lists the syntax, parameters, and switches for network commands

RUNNING APPLICATIONS IN THE COMMAND PROMPT WINDOW

You can install applications from the Command Prompt window, and you can run MS-DOS and Windows applications in the Command Prompt window. To run a program from the Command Prompt, follow these steps:

1. From the desktop, open the Start menu; choose Programs, and then choose the Command Prompt. The Command Prompt window appears.

2. If necessary, use the cd command to change to the directory holding the program you want to start. For example, to change to the WordPerfect directory, type **cd\wp60** and press Enter.

3. At the prompt, enter the program name that starts the program (for example, you'd type **wp** to start WordPerfect).

MS-DOS Window? You can manipulate a Command Prompt window similarly to other windows. In addition, check out the Control menu for other features.

COPYING AND PASTING FROM THE COMMAND PROMPT WINDOW

You can select text or graphics in any application open in the Command Prompt window, and you can copy or cut it and paste it into another application or document. Using the Copy and Paste procedures, you can copy data from one MS-DOS program and paste it into another MS-DOS program or a Windows application.

To copy and paste data, follow these steps:

1. In the Command Prompt window, open the application and the document from which you want to copy data.

2. Select the data to copy using the Edit, Mark command and click the Command Prompt window's Control menu button.

3. Select Edit, Copy. Windows NT copies the data to the Windows Clipboard (described in Lesson 9, "Copying and Moving Information Between Windows").

4. Switch to the window of the application and document to which you want to paste the copied data. You can use the taskbar to switch to either a Windows application or an application in another Command Prompt window.

5. Position the insertion point in the location where you want to add the data, and then choose Edit, Paste. (If the application is in a Command Prompt window, click the Control menu button and choose Edit, Paste instead.)

In this lesson, you learned to start and quit the Command
Prompt, enter commands at the Command Prompt, access online
help from the Command Prompt, and start an application from
the Command Prompt. In the next lesson, you'll learn to customize the appearance of Windows NT.

25

LESSON 25

CONTROLLING THE APPEARANCE OF WINDOWS NT

In this lesson, you'll learn to change desktop colors, add wallpaper and patterns to your desktop, and use a screen saver.

OPENING THE CONTROL PANEL

You use the *Control Panel* to control such aspects of Windows NT as the colors, fonts, modems, sounds, and so on. Figure 25.1 shows the Control Panel window; some of your icons may differ from those in the Figure 25.1.

FIGURE 25.1   Control your hardware, sounds, colors, and so on using the Control Panel icons.

To open the Control Panel, follow these steps:

1. Choose the Start button.

2. Select the Settings menu, Control Panel. To open any icon in the Control Panel, double-click that icon.

CHANGING THE COLOR SCHEME

You can change the color scheme that Windows NT uses for your desktop, windows, menus, title bars, and so on, to a preset color scheme. To change the Windows NT color scheme, follow these steps:

1. In the Control Panel, open the Display icon by double-clicking it.

2. Choose the Appearance tab. Figure 25.2 shows the Display Properties dialog box with the Appearance tab displayed.

FIGURE 25.2   Use the tabs in the Display Properties dialog box to control the features pertaining to the desktop.

3. From the Scheme drop-down list, select a color scheme. The sample at the top of the dialog box shows what the new colors in the windows and desktop will look like.

4. Check out as many different color schemes as you want. When you're satisfied with the selected color scheme, click OK. If you plan to make other changes to the Display Properties dialog box (in other tabs), choose the Apply button to accept the changes made to the Appearance tab and continue.

Default Colors If you want to go back to the scheme originally on your computer, choose Windows Standard if you've already made a change. If you have not made a change and you don't want to, choose Cancel.

ADDING WALLPAPER AND PATTERNS

You can choose from a variety of designs to apply to your desktop using the Desktop icon in the Control Panel. Figure 25.3 shows the Background tab of the Display Properties dialog box and its options.

FIGURE 25.3   Use the Background tab to add wallpaper or patterns to your desktop.

ADDING WALLPAPER

Wallpaper consists of colorful, *bitmapped images* that you display on your desktop for decoration.

Bitmapped Images   Bitmap is a file type used for storing certain images. Because the image is stored as a series of dots, called *pixels*, the image has rough edges and shows few details.

To apply a wallpaper design to your desktop, follow these steps:

1. In the Display Properties dialog box, choose the Background tab.

2. In the Wallpaper section, scroll the list and select the wallpaper design you want to use.

3. Click the Center option button to have Windows center one small icon from the file in the center of the desktop screen. Click the Tile option button to have Windows repeat the wallpaper icon so that the entire desktop is filled with the pattern.

4. Choose OK to close the dialog box and accept the wallpaper design. Alternatively, click the Apply button to accept this change and continue making changes to the Display Properties dialog box.

Why So Slow?   If you notice that your computer reacts more slowly than it did before, that's because using wallpaper and patterns for your desktop requires extra memory. If you're low on memory, you may want to use only a solid color for your desktop.

ADDING PATTERNS

Patterns are additional designs you can apply to your desktop for decoration. To apply a pattern, follow these steps:

1. In the Display Properties dialog box, choose the Background tab.

2. In the Pattern area of the dialog box, scroll the list and choose the pattern you want to use.

3. (Optional) Choose the Edit Pattern button and change the pattern by clicking the mouse in the pattern box. As you add to the design, the Sample box changes to reflect your additions. To remove an addition, click the box a second time. Choose Change to accept the changes and Done to close the Edit Pattern dialog box. If you do not want to save your changes, choose Done and when prompted to save, choose No.

4. Choose OK to close the Display Properties dialog box. The pattern appears on your desktop.

You Can't Use Both   If you select both a pattern and a wallpaper in the Desktop dialog box, the wallpaper overlays the pattern.

Adding a Screen Saver

Even though screen savers are no longer needed to prevent damage to your monitor from *burn-in*, they're still fun to use. If you select a screen saver, Windows runs a pattern across your screen anytime your computer is inactive for the specified length of time. To return to the screen and continue working, press a key or move the mouse.

To select a screen saver, follow these steps:

1. In the Display Properties dialog box, choose the Screen Saver tab. Figure 25.4 shows the Screen Saver tab of the Display Properties dialog box.

2. In the Screen Saver section, open the drop-down list and choose a screen saver.

Burn In   In older monitors, extremely light screens (such as those you see in Windows) had what is called a burn-in effect. When a Windows screen was left on the computer for a long period of time, the Windows image etched into the monitor's phosphors. Then when the monitor was turned off or used in DOS, a ghost of the Windows screen remained. Screen savers were originally used to lessen the burn-in effect. Newer monitors have built-in protection against burn-in.

FIGURE 25.4   Change screen savers periodically, just for fun.

3. Click the Preview button to view a sample of the screen saver to make sure you like it. When you finish viewing the screen saver, click the mouse button to return to the Desktop dialog box.

4. In the Delay text box, enter the number of minutes you want Windows NT to wait for your computer to be inactive before it starts the screen saver.

5. (Optional) Choose Password Protected if you want your screen saver to remain onscreen until you enter your password. This prevents other individuals from viewing your screen without your knowledge.

6. (Optional) Choose the Settings button to set any specific options that deal with your selected screen saver. Then choose OK to close the Settings dialog box.

7. Choose OK to close the dialog box and accept the changes. The next time you leave your computer inactive for the specified amount of time, the screen saver you selected appears onscreen.

In this lesson, you learned to change your desktop colors, add wallpaper and patterns to your desktop, and use a screen saver. In the next lesson, you'll learn to control some hardware settings (including setting the date and time and configuring your modem).

CONTROLLING HARDWARE SETTINGS

26

In this lesson, you'll learn to change the date and time and modify mouse and modem settings.

ALTERING THE DATE AND TIME

You use the Control Panel to set your computer's system date and time, which is used to time-stamp files as you create and modify them. In addition, many applications allow you to automatically insert the date and time onscreen or when you print, so you'll want to be sure to have the right time on your computer.

 Bad Battery? If you set your date and time, and then find that the date is wrong when you start your computer again, you probably have a bad battery.

To check or set the date and time, follow these steps:

1. From the desktop, open the Start menu, choose Settings and Control Panel.

2. In the Control Panel window, double-click the Date/Time icon. The Date/Time Properties dialog box appears with the Date & Timer tab selected (see Figure 26.1).

3. In the Date area, select the correct month and year from the drop-down lists; then click the day on the calendar.

4. To change the time, click the portion of the time you want to change and either enter the correct number or use the spinner arrows to increase or decrease the value accordingly.

FIGURE 26.1   The Date/Time Properties dialog box.

5. (Optional) Choose the Time Zone tab and check the Automatically Adjust for Daylight Savings Changes check box (put a check mark in it) if you want Windows to change the time automatically in the fall and spring.

6. Click OK or press Enter to accept the changes you have made. Click Cancel or press Esc to close the dialog box without saving changes.

 Time Zone   If necessary, use the Time Zone drop-down list to change your current time zone. You might use this option if you move or travel with your computer.

MODIFYING MOUSE SETTINGS

The mouse settings enable you to change tracking, to choose a double-click speed, and to swap the left and right mouse buttons. Figure 26.2 shows the Mouse Properties dialog box.

FIGURE 26.2   Adjust the mouse settings to better suit your needs.

By double-clicking the Mouse icon in the Control Panel, you access the Mouse Properties dialog box, where you can modify the following settings for your mouse:

Pointer Speed   (Motion tab) Use pointer speed when you're working on a notebook or laptop computer. The speed adjusts the rate at which the pointer travels across the screen, making it easier to find your pointer on the small screen. Set the speed to Slow if you have trouble seeing the mouse pointer; set the speed to Fast if the "slow-motion" mouse is distracting.

Pointer Trail   (Motion tab) If you use a notebook or laptop computer, you can choose to display a trail, or echo the pointer, to help you find the pointer on a small, poor-resolution screen. Choose Short for a brief trail or Long for an extended trail.

Double Click Speed   (Buttons tab) Adjust the speed to suit your finger's double-click speed. Slower means you can actually perform the two clicks more slowly. Adjust the speed, and then test it in the Test area.

Swap Left/Right Buttons   (Buttons tab) Check this box to switch buttons, if you're left-handed or just more comfortable with the switch.

Use the Pointers Tab   The Pointers tab of the Mouse Properties dialog box enables you to change your mouse pointers to look like dinosaurs, hands, and other icons. To view the different icon types, select an item from the Scheme drop-down list. Icons in the sample box change to reflect the selected scheme.

To modify the mouse settings, follow these steps:

1. From the desktop, open the Start menu and choose Settings, Control Panel.

2. In the Control Panel window, double-click the Mouse icon to open the Mouse Properties dialog box.

3. Adjust the settings.

4. Select OK or press Enter to accept the changes you have made. Select Cancel or press Esc to close the dialog box without saving changes.

CONFIGURING YOUR MODEM

If you have a modem attached to your computer, you can modify the settings. Additionally, you can add or remove modems easily using the Modem Wizard.

ADDING A MODEM

Before adding a modem, connect the modem to your machine, if it's external, and turn it on. If you've added an internal modem, make sure it's properly connected.

To add a modem, follow these steps:

1. From the desktop, open the Start menu and choose Settings, Control Panel.

2. Double-click the Modem icon to open the Modems Properties dialog box (see Figure 26.3)

FIGURE 26.3   Configure your modem in the Modems Properties dialog box.

3. To add a new modem, choose the Add button. The Install New Modem dialog box appears, as shown in Figure 26.4.

FIGURE 26.4   Adding a modem is as easy as following directions.

4. Let NT detect your modem by choosing the Next button; then follow the directions onscreen to complete the installation.

When NT returns to the Modems Properties dialog box, you can configure the dialing properties, as described in the next section, or you can choose the Close button to return to the desktop.

Too Many Modems? To remove a modem you no longer use, open the Modems Properties dialog box and select the modem from the list. Choose the Remove button. Choose Close to return to the desktop.

MODIFYING DIALING PROPERTIES

Dialing properties control how your calls are dialed. You may never need to modify these properties; however, if you're using a notebook and you use your modem from the road, hotels, and so on, you'll want to change dialing properties when you change locations.

To modify dialing properties

1. In the Modems Properties dialog box, choose the Dialing Properties tab.

2. In the Dialing Properties dialog box, choose the My Locations tab, as shown in Figure 26.5.

FIGURE 26.5 Use dialing properties when you go on the road with your notebook computer.

3. In the Where I Am area of the dialog box, enter the ZIP code and country from which you are calling.

4. In the How I Dial From This Location, enter the following information, as required:

> **To Access An Outside Line**   If you must first dial a number to access an outside line (as is often required in hotels), enter that number in this area; note you can enter a number to dial to access a local or long distance line.

> **Dial Using Calling Card**   Choose the Change button to enter your calling card number, if you want to use a card when dialing from this location.

> **This Location Has Call Waiting**   If the location from which you're calling has call waiting, enter the code to disable that feature while you're calling with a modem.

> **The Phone System At This Location Uses** Choose either Tone or Pulse dialing.

> **Come Here Often?**   If this is a location you often make modem calls from, you can save these settings for the next time you need to make a call. At the top of the dialog box, choose the New button. The text in the I Am Dialing From text box becomes selected; enter the location name to save it. Press Enter to accept the changes and close the dialog box.

5. Choose OK to accept the changes and close the dialog box; choose Close to close the Modems Properties dialog box.

CHANGING MODEM PROPERTIES

You also can modify certain modem settings as port, speed, and connection from the Modems Properties dialog box. Figure 26.6 shows a Hayes modem Properties dialog box; although each modem will have similar settings, the Properties boxes representing each brand or type of modem may look slightly different.

FIGURE 26.6   Make changes to your modem's configuration.

To change modem properties, follow these steps:

1. In the Modems Properties dialog box, select the modem you are configuring from the list so the modem's name is highlighted.

2. Choose the Properties button. Make any changes as follows:

   Port   Choose the port to which your modem is connected, usually a COM (communications) port.

   Speaker Volume   A personal preference; in most cases, you can turn the speaker volume off and adjust the volume. The sounds that come through the speaker are communication sounds between your modem and another; you can tell when the modems connect by listening to the sounds.

   Maximum Speed   Set the highest speed at which your modem can communicate. Your modem will adjust speed if the modem to which you're connecting runs at a slower speed.

   Connection Preferences   (on the Connections tab). These include data bits, parity, and stop bits settings. See the documentation of your ISP, BBS, or other network you're trying to connect to for this information.

Call Preferences   Choose whether to wait for a dial tone before dialing, the amount of time to wait before disconnecting if nothing is sent back and forth between the modems, and the amount of time to wait before canceling the call if connection doesn't take place.

 Questions?   If you have any questions about your modem's configuration, read the documentation that came with it.

3. Choose OK when finished setting the modem's properties. Choose Close to exit the Modems Properties dialog box.

In this lesson, you learned to change the date and time, modify mouse settings, and configure your modem.

INSTALLATION TROUBLESHOOTING

During the installation of Windows NT Workstation, you might run into some potential roadblocks. For example, you might be asked for some hardware information that you do not readily know, or you might run into some problems with the installation itself. This appendix offers some help for installing Windows NT Workstation.

WHAT YOU NEED TO KNOW

To save time during installation and to avoid frustration, gather the facts you need before you begin the installation. The inside front cover of this book gives you the basic steps for installing Windows NT Workstation, but there is much more to it than just those few steps. If you have any doubts, ask your system administrator. You will need all the following information in order to install Windows NT Workstation:

- The type of network adapter card you have, as well as the card's interrupt request number (IRQ) and base I/O (Input/Output) address will be very important. Consult the documentation that came with your network card for this information.

- Your computer name and workgroup or domain name.

- The printer model and the port to which it's connected (if you have a printer connected directly to your computer).

- Whether you want to create a dual boot and preserve the existing operating system within a partition or reformat the drive to a Windows NT Workstation operating system is important. You can designate a portion (partition) of the drive as MS-DOS and a portion as Windows NT. Your decision depends on the type of programs you use, your network logons, and other factors. If you're unsure, see your system administrator.

- Which network protocols to install to be compatible to the network to which you're attached.

 Floppy Disk   You will need a high-density floppy disk on which to create an emergency repair disk during Windows NT installation. You can use the disk later to repair Windows NT if you have a problem with the program.

INSTALLING WINDOWS NT WORKSTATION FROM A CD

After you complete the installation steps in the inside front cover of this book, you begin installing Windows NT Workstation using either a CD-ROM or Setup disk 4. The first problem may occur if NT Setup prompts for Setup disk 4 instead of reading your CD-ROM. If this happens, it means that your CD-ROM device is not a supported device. Windows NT supports only SCSI CD-ROM devices. If your CD-ROM is not a SCSI, you must install Windows NT Workstation in a different way.

If your CD-ROM device is supported in MS-DOS, you can install Windows NT Workstation from MS-DOS. If you do, your drive will use dual boot and the FAT file system instead of the NTFS. FAT (File Allocation Table file system) and NTFS (NT File System) are two different methods operating systems use to organize the files on disk. The NTFS system offers more security options when used with Windows NT. Your network and your system administrator will probably have a preference for the type of file system you use, so you should ask him or her before you install Windows NT. Alternatively, you can install Windows NT Workstation from the network. Ask your system administrator for more information.

To install Windows NT using an unsupported CD-ROM device, follow these steps:

1. Exit Setup by following the directions onscreen. Prepare three formatted high-density disks you can use during setup, plus an extra disk for an emergency repair disk. Label the disks Setup boot disk, Setup disk #2, Setup disk #3, and Emergency Repair disk.

2. In MS-DOS, insert the Windows NT Workstation CD-ROM into the CD-ROM drive. At the MS-DOS prompt, type the CD-ROM drive letter and the directory name **I386**. For example, if your CD-ROM drive letter is **D**, type **D:\I386** and press Enter.

3. At the prompt, type **winnt** and press Enter. The CD-ROM begins setup. During setup, you will be prompted to insert each floppy disk in turn. Windows NT Workstation Setup copies files to the floppy disks and to your hard disk.

4. When it finishes copying files, Setup asks you to press Enter to restart the computer. Press Enter.

5. The computer reboots, and Setup asks you to insert the Setup boot disk. When you do, Setup begins installation of the Windows NT Workstation files. Follow directions onscreen to complete the installation.

No CD-ROM Drive?!   Windows NT will not recognize your CD-ROM drive after installation if the drive is not supported. You might be able to acquire an updated driver that will work with Windows NT from the drive's manufacturer.

Troubleshooting Installation

You could run into a host of hardware or software problems during installation. These are just a few of the possibilities, along with some suggestions that might make for a smoother installation. As always, if you need more help, see your system administrator.

IRQ CONFLICTS

Interrupt conflicts are problems that occur when two hardware devices are trying to share the same IRQ settings. It is important to keep notes on the IRQ settings each component of your computer uses to ensure that you don't assign the same address to two devices. Generally, Windows NT Workstation Setup will suggest settings and identify conflicts. However, if a device does not seem to be working, you'll want to check your settings to make sure there are no conflicts. You can find out a hardware's settings by referring to that hardware's documentation.

PROBLEMS WITH FAX/MODEMS OR OTHER DEVICES

Some peripherals (such as a non-SCSI CD-ROM device) may not be supported by Windows NT Workstation and, therefore, may not work. You can contact the manufacturer of the device to see if they have an updated driver that works with Windows NT.

DISPLAYS, DRIVERS, AND MONITORS

At one point during the installation of Windows NT Workstation, Setup asks you about your monitor's resolution. Be very careful when changing options in that Setup dialog box. Windows NT suggests a configuration and asks you to test it. If you do not have a good reason to change the configuration, and the test looks okay to you, do not change anything in the dialog box.

If you change drivers and you choose the wrong one for your video card, your computer may not restart correctly. If that happens, choose the VGA boot option on the Boot Loader starting screen, and then manually set the video driver in the Control Panel. You may need to ask for assistance from your system administrator.

APPENDIX B

SETTING UP THE INTERNET EXPLORER

Setting up Windows NT to use the Internet Explorer is not an easy task. You must install the protocol as well as Dial-Up Networking, and you'll need to find out the settings for your Internet service provider's server, IP address, and so on. This lesson introduces you to the steps you need to complete to prepare to use the Internet Explorer; however, you may need more help before you're ready to connect.

Help!   For more help on getting ready to connect to the Internet, check out the online help in NT. Search for Internet in the Help Index then click connecting to.

Before you connect to the Internet, you need to complete the tasks outlined in the following general steps:

1. Connect and then install a modem to your computer (or access to a modem over your network). Set up a modem in the Control Panel by double-clicking the Modem icon and following directions to the Add Modem Wizard.

2. Get an Internet account with an Internet service provider (ISP). You'll need to know the following: username, password, access phone number, the host's name and domain name, the Domain Name Server (DNS) server address, IP address, authentication procedure, Subnet Mask, and Default Gateway. Choose a PPP (Point-to-Point) account, if your provider offers it.

3. Install the TCP/IP protocol to your workstation from the Control Panel, Network icon. In the Protocols tab, choose

the Add button and select the TCP/IP protocol. When prompted to use the DHCP to configure the TCP/IP protocol automatically, choose Yes.

4. In the Network dialog box, Protocols tab, choose the TCP/IP Protocol and select the Properties button. In the IP Address tab, choose to Specify an IP Address and fill in the information as given to you by your ISP (see Figure B.1). Choose OK when you are finished. You'll be prompted to restart your computer, but wait; there are other settings to configure first.

FIGURE **B.1**   Fill in the information for your Internet server.

 IP Addresses? Subnet Mask?   The configuration settings you enter into the Dial-Up Networking and TCP/IP Properties dialog boxes are each unique. The numbers, separated by periods, identify the network to which the server is attached and the server itself.

5. Install Dial-Up Networking, if it is not already installed. In the Control Panel, use the Add/Remove Programs icon to install Dial-Up Networking. You'll need the Windows

NT Workstation CD-ROM to complete installation. When next you're prompted to restart the computer, do so.

6. In My Computer, double-click the Dial-Up Networking icon and follow the directions for setting up your connection to the access provider. You'll need to know the ISP's phone number, server type, whether you'll need a terminal window to log on, and so on. Figure B.2 shows the completed Dial-Up Networking dialog box.

FIGURE B.2   You're ready to dial your Internet service.

  Trouble?   If you have trouble connecting to your Internet service and you need to edit settings, choose the More button in the Dial-Up Networking dialog box and select Edit Entry and Modem Properties

INDEX